D1316756

FROM GESTURE TO IDEA: ESTHETICS AND ETHICS IN MOLIÈRE'S COMEDY

NATHAN GROSS

FROM GESTURE TO IDEA:
ESTHETICS AND ETHICS
IN MOLIÈRE'S COMEDY

1982
COLUMBIA UNIVERSITY PRESS
NEW YORK

Library of Congress Cataloging in Publication Data

Gross, Nathan.
From gesture to idea—esthetics and ethics
in Molière's comedy.

Includes bibliographical references and
index.

1. Molière, 1622-1673—Criticism and
interpretation. I. title.
PQ1860.G7   842'.4   82-4271
ISBN 0-231-05440-8   AACR2

Columbia University Press
New York   Guildford, Surrey

Book design by Ken Venezio

Title page art by Kléber Carpentier

In memory of

NATHAN EDELMAN

CONTENTS

ACKNOWLEDGMENTS

These essays took shape mostly in 1972–73 during a sabbatical leave spent in Paris and in 1975–76 during residence at the Camargo Foundation in Cassis, France. It is a pleasure to record my gratitude to the foundation for its hospitality and to those friends and colleagues who provided cheer and unstinting moral support—esthetics and ethics—during various visits to Paris since 1972: Carl Viggiani, Ed and Alma Law, Joseph Ianella, Dick Arndt, Rusty Park, and especially Lilia Tchistoganow. Many associates at Columbia University provided pointers and encouragement, often unbeknownst to them, by chance remarks, but more often by example of character through their behavior: the late Lawton P. G. Peckham, William Theodore deBary, Bernard Friedman, Leon and Jacqueline Roudiez, Robert Belknap, Edna White, Charles Potter, Peter Shamonsey, Elena Sansalone. Participating in the Humanities Program of Columbia College has allowed me the delightful privilege of thinking out loud on the great philosophical texts, from Homer to Dostoevsky in the traditional syllabus and occasionally beyond, in the company of the intellectually curious and sometimes intimidatingly brilliant young minds that Columbia College continues to attract—and with reason, if my colleagues on the Humanities staff from year to year are typical of their instructors. I am particularly grateful to a former student in Humanities, William Germano, assistant executive editor at Columbia University Press, whose curiosity about the long-promised manuscript on Molière encouraged me to revise to my satisfaction at last an introduction summarizing and bringing focus to the philosophical issues underlying the group of essays. Jules Brody, now at Harvard University, was my first teacher of Molière at Columbia College; his advice has been instrumental at every stage of my career, as it was in my choice of the Johns Hopkins University for graduate study. There I was privileged to attend Bruce Wardropper's seminars in Spanish literature—models of exploration, elucidation, and elegance that reflected both the man and the scholar. There too was the late Nathan Edelman, whose integrity, patience, and *bonté* have sustained my desire to withhold these essays, despite the well-known and very real pressures to publish, until they seemed to me as close to his standards as I may reasonably approach. I finally commit them to print, certain that he would have received them with his customary kindness, wit, and gracious—graceful, too—acceptance of their inevitable shortcomings.

FROM GESTURE TO IDEA: ESTHETICS AND ETHICS IN MOLIÈRE'S COMEDY

INTRODUCTION

Each of these essays on Molière's comedy develops from the observation of a specific detail of language and gesture, more apparent in a staged performance than in a reading of the printed text, into an exploration of the underlying ethical values that the play in question urges upon an audience's attention. The point of departure is an awareness of a significant repeated element in the esthetic design of each drama, whose structure follows readily discernible patterns not only of plot and language, but also of physical movement and gesture readily extrapolated by an actor or director from indications in the spoken lines.

Molière's own preference for a highly gestural style in his company's productions is indicated by the occurence of farce in plays from every stage of his career. A performance of the early farce *Le Docteur amoureux* in 1658 before the young Louis XIV earned for Molière the use of the theater in the Salle du Petit-Bourbon attached to the Louvre. He shared it with an Italian commedia dell'arte troupe which, performing in a foreign language before a French audience, of necessity expressed the entire range of human passions mostly by gestural means. In his late farce *Les Fourberies de Scapin* (1671), Molière rendered admiring and grateful tribute to his Italian colleagues, sustained contact with whom had permitted a significant refinement of the cruder style apparent in the farces composed before 1658 during his peregrinations in the provinces. These plays belong to native French traditions that Molière knew from his childhood in Paris, where rough-and-tumble farce might be seen, for example, on the Pont-Neuf, at various outdoor fairs, and at the two permanent indoor theaters. Molière subsequently developed a style combining the French tradition, with its typical characters and gestures, and the more sophisticated Italian farce, thus joining a native, popular, and basically medieval genre to one whose roots reached back to the literature of the Italian Renaissance and ultimately to the quintessential European comedy of Terence and Plautus and the New Comedy of Menander.

Molière's exaggerated, but stylized, mannerisms in performance are documented by contemporary accounts of his portrayal of Arnolphe in *L'École des femmes*, his first full-scale five-act comedy in verse; in the farce of *Le Médecin malgré lui*, stage directions printed right in the text indicate the degree of gesture used to provoke laughter. Elements of physical farce intrude into even the most serious of plays, like *Le Misanthrope* (in the bumblings of Alceste's servant at the end of act IV) and *Les Femmes savantes* (where the lackey cannot move a chair without taking a tumble). In the comédies-ballets, entertainments devised for royal festivities, they also furnish a basis for many of the danced interludes, some of which are accompanied by songs or chants in foreign or macaronic languages— a verbal equivalent of farce—as in the initiation ceremonies of *Le Bourgeois gentilhomme* and *Le Malade imaginaire*.

The emphasis in farce on what is seen as distinguished from what is heard also contributes in an extremely refined and concentrated form to the conception of character in the major plays. Molière seems to have imagined many of the protagonists in those grandes comédies less as abstract types or masks than as individuals whose defects emerge not only in their intentions but also in idiosyncratic vocabulary and distinctive physical movement. For example, the misanthrope recoils as he shuns offers of friendship and as he disdainfully isolates himself in a corner from the other visitors to the salon; the miser, who is wracked by fits of coughing, grasps at other characters to search for suspected theft and seizes even himself at the comic climax when he discovers his strongbox has disappeared.

These gestures recur within episodes of plot arranged in parallel cycles. Organization of the dramatic text by the playwright—an important aspect of the esthetic control that distinguishes French classicism—guides the spectator's pleasurable response; it furnishes a series of contexts that allow him, by virtue of his knowledge of similar earlier incident, vocabulary, and gesture, to anticipate the comic protagonist's behavior and to appreciate ironies of situation and language. A model of such structural manipulation, amounting to a delightful complicity between poet and audience, is *L'École des femmes*, whose turns of plot foster expectations of recurrent reversals in Arnolphe's plans. His pretensions of omniscience and power are consistently exposed and exploded, as each successive episode deflates his swollen ego and defeats his selfish intentions, usually because, ironically, he acts on the basis of faulty assumptions. Not the least of his errors concerns his ward's identity, for Agnès is no peasant's child, contrary to his statement early in the play, but, as he learns in the last scene, an heiress and the niece of his own best friend, Chrysalde. Each episode reflects this passage from assumptions of knowledge, based on both appearances and wishful thinking, to truth—from ignorance to revelation—which governs the action of the play.

The conclusion fully satisfies the audience: we have learned from experience (unlike the protagonist) to expect Arnolphe to pass suddenly from arrogant confidence to dismay as bits of information are innocently offered him by Agnès or by Horace, whose speeches provide a second version of some event Arnolphe has narrated, mostly to his own satisfaction. This structural device of *récits*—narrative speeches—affords the audience a pleasure that derives from the immediate satisfaction of witnessing the frustration Arnolphe deserves as punishment for his injustice and insensitivity. But the dual *récits* also provide reminders that he has been somewhat less than honest in his accounts and that some crucial fact has escaped his awareness. For instance, Horace's only speech in act IV, recounting Arnolphe's appearance in Agnès' room, dwells upon Arnolphe's violent behavior, which Arnolphe had not previously mentioned, and upon Horace's own hidden presence in a closet. The dual narratives taken together constitute an esthetic device that du-

3

plicates the discrepancy between the overall action of the play and Arnolphe's lifelong project to marry Agnès: what Arnolphe sees in his own behavior and in Agnès' origins and docile character—"un air doux et posé" that he had observed in her as an infant—does not correspond to fact. Molière has constructed not a comedy of errors but a comedy of ignorance, in which, at every turn of plot—that is, at every *récit*—the audience learns that Arnolphe knows nothing, either of the essential truths that lie at the heart of human nature and behavior, or of the very situations he himself has brought about and believes he controls.

Arnolphe's ego does not survive the ultimate revelation of truth contained in a final *récit* that Molière distributes in couplets between two characters on either side of Arnolphe, at whom he must look by turns in growing stunned bewilderment and rage. His final cry of "Ouf!"—as Molière in performance altered the "Oh!" of the printed text—is literally a deflated man's last gasp that completes the pattern of action and produces in the audience a pleasure grown from the comedy's global structural arrangement. Those contemporary critics who took Molière to task for the prevalence of long narratives in the play and whom Molière answers in *La Critique de L'École des femmes* were perhaps not ready for the classical control of plot and shaping of the audience's pleasurable responses that Molière had brought to the five-act comedy. Or, like Arnolphe, perhaps they were simply unable to cope with another man's art and success.

The comic effect of *L'École des femmes* is supported by verbal and ironic devices which promote enjoyment locally, as it were, at each episode. Such amusement emanates less often from gratuitous word-play, like Shakespearean wit and punning or Aristophanic verbal fantasy, than from repeated phrases and cumulative patterns that amount to comic turns in contexts elaborated expressly for that purpose. Harpagon's "Sans dot!" and Orgon's "Le pauvre homme!", although not necessarily funny in themselves, produce laughter in context by dint of repetition. The audience delights in ironic interplay, particularly when the context permits the ironist himself to become the victim of irony, wittingly or otherwise. Such pleasure is especially marked in *L'École des femmes*, where, for instance, of the characters Arnolphe alone perceives and enjoys the equivocal nature of his remarks to Agnès:

AR: Vous vous êtes toujours, comme on voit, bien portée?
AG: Hors les puces, qui m'ont la nuit inquiétée.
AR: *Ah! vous aurez dans peu quelqu'un pour les chasser.*
AG: Vous me ferez plaisir.
AR: *Je le puis bien penser.*

But he fails to discern the unintended allusion to little horns and cuckoldry—precisely what he fears and what he is always on the lookout for in other men—in her description of the handiwork he takes to be a sign of her innocence and docility:

AR: Que faites-vous donc là?
AG: *Je me fais des cornettes.*
Vos chemises de nuit et *vos coiffes sont faites.*

(I, iii, 235–40; italics added)

The jokes occurring in catch phrases or in ironies of language set into a limited context always function additionally, however, to indicate the protagonist's ethical defect. Their phrases point to Harpagon's avarice and to Orgon's wish to consider Tartuffe, despite all the evidence of his sensual satisfactions, a miserable, helpless creature in need of salvation by Orgon, while Arnolphe's insensitivity to the possibility of unexpected or unintentional meanings in his innocent ward's behavior or language is indicative of the arrogance and ignorance that consistently prove his undoing. It is typical of French classicism that every self-contained pleasing detail—in this case, every joke, gesture, or structural element which produces laughter—should reflect the overall esthetic design and contribute to the spectator's awareness of the principal question of values informing the work as a whole.

In Molière's comedy the gesture leads to an idea, and esthetics leads to ethics, to considerations of the ideology, or mythology, governing behavior in the spectator's culture and guaranteeing its

validity. The comic protagonist's idiosyncratic or perverse interpretation deforms an essential element of the ideology and threatens
the institutions based upon it. Ultimately at issue in these plays is
the conservation of the culture itself and its values, as the audience
reaffirms its acquiescence and fidelity to the ideology supporting
authoritative institutions and hierarchical relationships within the
culture. These institutions might be considered in Platonic terms
as reflections of the Ideas that the society attempts to reproduce,
and the drama itself might be described as an imitation or representation not only of human beings in action, as the Aristotelian
formula puts it, but of the Ideas determining the institutions and
relationships, indeed the underlying values, prevalent in the culture.
The function of poetry—should Socrates agree to admit the right
kind of poetry to his Republic—must lie in the reminders it furnishes
of the Good, or of whatever archetypal values the philosopher-king
mediating between Ideas and community may consider appropriate
to communal well-being and to the optimal fulfillment as a human
being of each participant in the community. Molière's comedy, as
part of that classical literature which knows neither temporal nor
spatial limits, affords such images of the Ideas that shape all aspects
of human relationships in the civilized state: the stage picture of
movement and gesture and the intellectual tableau formed by words
combine to allow the audience a glimpse of the Idea as perceived in
the poet's mirror.

Aristotle's discussion of drama may also be appreciated within a
Platonic optic. Strictly speaking, the poetry he analyzes imitates no
real human beings: the representation of their actions belongs to the
category of history. The plot, or *mythos*, is a fiction which refers to
some truth posited within the ideological system and serves as a
reminder of that system itself. It depicts images of probability: such
events might have happened and might presumably befall members
of the audience. The convention of probability operates on the basis
of prevailing beliefs about a universal human nature—physical,
emotional, intellectual—as well as accepted notions concerning the
nature of the physical world and that of a postulated moral order.

The assumption that all men share the same qualities and defects explains the drama's ability to arouse sympathetic responses in a spectator who recognizes in the protagonist a man like himself and in the represented myth a projection of his own capacity for behavior and the consequences of that behavior, given both his character, which must be formed from the universal qualities and vices, and his potential failure, equal to the protagonist's, to discern the full implications of his acts in the context of a vast, mostly unknowable universe in which, he believes, a moral order supervised by divine forces remains mysterious.

The forms of dramatic poetry, tragedy and comedy, produce on a spectator effects which differ according to the manner in which the play recalls the idea central to the culture's mythology. In both forms the idea of man's place in the moral order—as perceived or dictated by the authoritative guardians or definers of that moral order in the culture—is ultimately reaffirmed after the protagonist has violated it. In tragedy the protagonist unknowingly commits dreadful acts, the thought of which is normally not to be acknowledged, much less uttered or otherwise brought into the open. As Freud observed, they are, nevertheless, deeds that men are dissuaded from performing by nothing less than the restraints of civilization and a consciousness of some retributive and conservative moral order inculcated with all the force of the authoritative myth defining culture. The tragic character acts out, as an involuntary example, those violent passions that spring from a universal desire for self-assertion over all threatening rivals for pleasure and power. We can thrill with terror and horror, experiencing "tragic pleasure," before the character's unwitting imitation of unspeakable acts whose possibility for ourselves we repress, and we can experience compassion for the hero who suffers and accepts—even chooses to suffer—the consequences of deeds unknowingly accomplished in violation of the moral law. Tragedy furnishes reminders of the idea of a moral order postulated by the authoritative mythology that makes the culture possible; tragedy also projects the idea of man as a being with limited capacities to know the moral order, who harbors unutterably horrible impulses that must be repressed lest the moral order be violated and the culture destroyed.

Respect for the inviolability of the moral order, mythological though it may be, is the condition for the culture's survival. The idea of moral order is prerequisite to that of culture itself; should the sanctity of the moral order be debased—should the mythology be challenged or exposed as a myth without substance—the civilization is threatened by collapse. Such exposure provides the material of classical history, not drama; it furnishes the plot of the model for all tragic history, Thucydides' account of the Peloponnesian War, a work in which the punishment of the violators of the moral order is insufficient to restore the civil order. Here is tragedy occurring in history and culminating in unmitigated disaster and chaos, for it lacks the reassertion of the moral order characteristic of tragic drama. Tragedy is a conservative form; it allows the spectator a cathartic outlet, an acting out in myth of what must not be expressed, much less performed, in history—within the spectator's own life and culture—lest the historical moment come to an abrupt end.

Comedy, of course, engenders laughter, not terror or compassion, even though the comic protagonist openly plans and engages in unspeakable actions that violate the moral order implicit in the culture's ideology. The audience derides and condemns him; but spectators may secretly approve or envy behavior which enacts repressed ambitions. In the preface to *Tartuffe* Molière restates the classical theory that the usefulness—the *emploi*—of comedy is to "corriger les vices des hommes" and that nothing better serves the purpose of reproving the majority of men than "la peinture de leurs défauts." Although few spectators would acknowledge as their own the peculiarities of Alceste, the sins of Dom Juan, or the avarice of Harpagon, Molière is proposing that all men are somehow depicted in such figures and that comedy produces its particular response because a bit of the comic protagonist lodges in every human being. The representation of his actions in the poem allows a harmless exercise of universal defects and, consequently, a correction (in all but incorrigible misfits) that adjusts the passions and all the more strongly subjects antisocial or criminal desires to the conservative law. This acting out is a catharsis intended to promote continued repression in support of the culture and the ideology underpinning it. "On veut bien être méchant; mais on ne veut point être ridicule." Unlike the protagonist—or hero, depending on one's perspective and attitudes—the spectator does not dare indulge secret desires branded as vices by the culture.

Nor does he, except through his harmless laughter, dare cast the first stone. For at moments of climax or stress, Molière's comedy may make the spectator suddenly aware of his own unjust behavior or unsympathetically harsh reactions: Orgon deserves the treatment he gets from Tartuffe; Argan's insensitivity toward his children and blindness to their stepmother's obvious machinations make us feel he deserves the doctor's curse (and even whatever sickness he may in fact suffer); it seems right that Harpagon lose his buried treasure. At those moments when his authority crumbles, and with it the possibility that his fantasies may be satisfied, our secret sympathy for, or envy of, the *paterfamilias-cum-tyrannos* vanishes, replaced by pleasure at his discomfiture. That pleasure, however, is problematic, for we may judge not according to strict universal or culturally mediated standards, but according to irrational instincts.

The outstanding example of this ad hoc justice occurs at Harpagon's direct appeal to the audience for information concerning his missing strongbox. Instead of agreeing that Harpagon's rights as owner of the treasure have in fact been violated and that, in a state governed by law enforced by just authorities, he is entitled to the restoration of his wealth, the audience ignores justice and law, preferring to substitute a primitive system of retribution: because Harpagon violates the most basic natural rights of his children, the violation of his rights of property is only fair treatment and appropriate punishment that is to be applauded. But even if Harpagon abuses his powers as a father and his prerogatives as a businessman, and even if he perversely misconstrues the idea underlying those rights, thereby violating law and threatening the culture, the spectator must not fall into the trap of imitating Harpagon's errors by forgetting the existence of law, to whose protection even the miser is entitled. We may collectively commit that error, as members of an audience witnessing a fiction; harmlessly acting out our instincts, we become aware of the dangers they pose. Molière sets the trap for us by arranging the action of the comedy to make the audience desire Harpagon's comeuppance; at every turn the miser proves the obstacle to the happiness of the likeable young characters. But Molière's dramaturgy serves the ethical purpose of bringing the audience up short, suddenly making us wonder about the legitimate, or otherwise, quality of our own behavior.

The failure of *L'Avare*, commonly attributed to its unusual form—a five-act comedy in prose, not the expected verse—may have resulted from the uneasiness it still produces, from the tension between, on the one hand, our knowledge that law must be universally and evenhandedly enforced, and, on the other hand, our more instinctual desire to apply a personal sense of right and wrong, reward and punishment. If we yield to such wishes, we act out, within our own real nonfictional being in history, one more distortion of the cultural values and the idea supporting them that the comedy seeks to reinforce in a form retaining as much integrity as possible.

Comedy leads the spectator, painlessly, but with some shock, to recognize and condemn within himself the inherent defects of which the protagonist's behavior is a figural representation. The play's esthetic devices guide the audience's reactions. They consistently draw attention to the protagonist's deliberate imposition of misconceptions that he insists reflect an accurate vision of the moral order. A spectator in secret sympathy with the protagonist's vice notices nonetheless the discrepancy between the officially sanctioned doctrine that he honors and the comic character's flawed account of it. For every comic protagonist exercises his vice and justifies his behavior, arguing with apparent logic from a specious principle that resembles, but in debased or distorted form, some assumption essential to the culture. His reasoning begins with an erroneous first principle since some unmentionable, unrepressed desire influences his perception of the moral order. He belongs to the class of "inferior men" deemed appropriate for comedy by Aristotle (*Poetics* 1449a), "inferior" referring, however, not to rank but to the distortion of his moral sense and to the manner in which he uses his mind.

Molière's protagonists—the brilliant aristocrats Dom Juan and Alceste; the bourgeois Arnolphe, Orgon, Harpagon and his image-in-reverse, Monsieur Jourdain; and the peasant George Dandin—all apply their intellect to justify the specious principles that they exercise in flawed behavior. Such argument, however logical in form it may seem, amounts to another kind of esthetic gesture by the characters that does not succeed in disguising the unethical nature of their essential thoughts and intentions. Their subjection of intellect to a perverse cause destructive of the culture makes them morally inferior to other characters, in particular to their wives (in the case of Orgon and Jourdain), to their commonsensical servants at the lower end of the social scale, and to the *raisonneurs*, whose exposition of ethical notions recalls the normal conservative view of the authoritative ideology. The comic character's actions, gestures, and arguments reflect his faulty vision and resemble a grotesque parody of behavior faithful to the idea governing relationships amongst civilized men. His abuse of intelligence—the faculty of reason that distinguishes human from beast—to serve some vice and commit the unspeakable in the name of some misconceived principle transforms him into an inferior, corrupt being in whom animal—i.e., precivilized—instincts prevail. The strategy of Molière's comedy finally allows him, and the spectator, the chance to admit his defect, inherent in human nature after the Fall, and to change his ways by properly exercising reason according to a first principle that is true to the moral order postulated by the culture. The workings in the play of esthetics, bringing about laughter and a painless focus on the comic protagonist's erroneous version of ethical principles, help persuade the spectator to use that opportunity for himself. The comic protagonist's conversion to ethical values genuinely reflecting the idea governing the culture remains problematic, however, as these essays will indicate.

· I ·

MORTIFICATION AND CHARITY IN *LE TARTUFFE*

Tartuffe's first brief speech is a concentrated version of the sequence mortification–charity which recurred in acts I and II during his absence from the stage:

Laurent, serrez ma haire avec ma discipline,
Et priez que toujours le Ciel vous illumine.
Si l'on vient pour me voir, je vais aux prisonniers
Des aumônes que j'ai partager les deniers.

(III, ii, 853–56)

The character who has been called both saint and hypocrite finally enters to summarize and virtually to personify the idea shaping the play. Tartuffe preaches mortification in severe penance for the self and the sharing in charity of worldly goods, obtained in this instance through begging, another form of mortification, with prisoners who, by the letter of the law, deserve no kindness. But a stage direction preceding his pronouncement, "apercevant Dorine," and her comment, "Que d'affectation et de forfanterie!" (857), suggest that his words constitute an insubstantial esthetic gesture and violate the principle that true Christians draw no attention to their works. Tartuffe's devout practices amount to misleading performances intended to persuade selected witnesses of his saintliness while in fact he lacks the commitment to Christian ethics and ideology such habits are expected to connote. That is the sense of his hypocrisy. Tartuffe's acts of mortification and charity also perversely misrepresent the bonds between man and God that form the basis of genuine religious attitudes and practice. Under the influence of this misrepresentation, Orgon attempts to subject his family to a rigorous discipline in penance for the abject worthlessness Tartuffe attributes to man, while Orgon himself is encouraged, as an authority crudely imitating God, to dispense charity in recompense to those who acknowledge their ethical nullity before his power and wisdom. Orgon rewards only Tartuffe, however, since the members of his household refuse the notion of their sinfulness from the outset in their confrontation with Madame Pernelle. They resist arbiters of behavior who misuse mortification and charity as instruments of tyranny. Tartuffe, Orgon, and Madame Pernelle offend noble, humanistic sensibilities—and the truly devout—because they imitate faithlessly, perversely, unjustly the Christian ideological model describing man's relation to God, which commands the fallible but not totally worthless creature to hope for a restoring grace freely bestowed by a loving, forgiving, bountiful power.

The sequence of mortification-and-charity occurs explicitly for the first time in Orgon's account of his initial encounters with Tartuffe in church.

Chaque jour à l'église il venait, d'un air doux,
Tout vis-à-vis de moi se mettre à deux genoux.
Il attirait les yeux de l'assemblée entière
Par l'ardeur dont au Ciel il poussait sa prière;
Il faisait des soupirs, de grands élancements,
Et baisait humblement la terre à tous moments;
Et lorsque je sortais, il me devançait vite,
Pour m'aller à la porte offrir de l'eau bénite.
Instruit par son garçon, qui dans tout l'imitait,
Et de son indigence, et de ce qu'il était,
Je lui faisais des dons; mais avec modestie
Il me voulait toujours en rendre une partie.
"C'est trop, me disait-il, c'est trop de la moitié;
Je ne mérite pas de vous faire pitié";
Et quand je refusais de le vouloir reprendre,
Aux pauvres, à mes yeux, il allait le répandre.

Enfin le Ciel chez moi me le fit retirer,
Et depuis ce temps-là tout semble y prospérer.

(I, v, 287–300)

In this narrative Tartuffe enters, as it were, in a position of prayer and mortification on his knees; but something in Orgon's phrasing seems peculiar: "Chaque jour à l'église il venait d'un air doux, / Tout vis-à-vis de moi se mettre à deux genoux." This "vis-à-vis," emphasized by the "tout," means ordinarily "opposite" or "next to," but literally "face to face." Tartuffe could not kneel literally "vis-à-vis" Orgon in a church where everyone prays toward an altar with a crucifix bearing a representation of divinity;[1] he must have knelt next to Orgon, or across an aisle, or even on the opposite side of an altar, in a chapel or in the transept, as is possible in baroque churches. But Orgon does not say "tout à côté de moi" or "tout près de moi": at the level of language revealing Orgon's desires—"in poetic" if not "in fact"—Tartuffe seems to face Orgon, while his gestures of mortification and worship seem addressed to Orgon, drawing attention to both of them and distracting from the service at the altar. Orgon countenances this improper, even perverse behavior which any Christian (or adherent to a religious ideology distinguishing man from divinity) might find offensive.

These implications would be reinforced were the gestural allusions in the speech to be acted out. A performer trained in the traditions of Italian commedia dell'arte, like Molière, would portray the scene as he narrated it; and any actor trying to enliven a long speech will revert to complementary gesture. The effect of this account would be accentuated if a crucifix were part of the stage décor, so that Orgon's imitations of Tartuffe might occur in the presence of an element of the altar. But it is unlikely that Molière could have shown

---

1. The significant exception to the normal direction of worship is worth noting: while the king faced the altar, courtiers turned toward him, as though the king, in the act of communicating with God in prayer on behalf of the entire kingdom, reflected the divinity and were himself an object of adoration.

a crucifix in the set representing a *salle basse* or common room of a devout bourgeois household in the Marais: the play would have been banned in 1669 for violation of religious sensibilities. In the version of Roger Planchon, however, produced in Lyons in 1974 and in Paris in 1975 and 1977, religious iconography is used effectively, even spectacularly, and the presence of representations of a suffering Christ-as-witness and a crucifix are no longer offensive. On the contrary, they underscore the point of this scene of mortification before another man who secretly desires a creature to acknowledge his superiority, the gap in value between himself and the self-humiliating man—a gap that is illusory and that cannot correspond to the abyss separating man from God. Before a crucifix on stage, Orgon's representation of Tartuffe's perverse, self-mortifying behavior in church makes the audience see in Orgon a man who, playing both parts, Orgon and Tartuffe, seems to worship . . . himself! He imitates a model of perverse religious behavior which deforms the very purpose of prayer, the acknowledgment of man's frailty before God, not vis-à-vis other human creatures. If there is a crucifix on stage, then Orgon acts out the scene in full view of the divinity, as it were, to whom prayers and acts of contrition such as mortification should be addressed.

Orgon's taking both parts also lends an air of farce to the episode. This contributes to the passage's offensive character—a serious act, mortification, is imitated by a man who changes roles and exaggerates, even in the next part of the sequence, whose subject is charity. Orgon rewards Tartuffe who offers him holy water, presumably from another position of humility on his knees. This act may seem gratuitous, for anyone may dip into the vessels and take holy water with which to genuflect toward the altar. But Tartuffe hurries ahead of Orgon to assume the position of one who mortifies himself as a servant furnishing the means of accomplishing a necessary sacramental act; his mortification is associated with Orgon's devotional exercise. Thus, vis-à-vis Orgon, Tartuffe is a penitent and an instrument of salvation. Orgon's response is immediately to reward this stranger. His alms, however, are like an immediate recompense, either for the sacramental water or for the flattering sense that Tartuffe has mortified himself before Orgon. Tartuffe has virtually invited Orgon to react in a manner analogous to the response to which the devout Christian hopes his God will be moved: charity for the fallen man who acknowledges his error and helplessness.

Acts of penitence, of which kneeling is a symbolic reflection during prayer before the superior power, are undertaken in the hope of being raised from the state of sin—from the death of the Fall—to eternal life. At its most basic level of meaning, penitence for the Christian evokes an archetype of death-and-resurrection: he mortifies himself in an acknowledgment of the worthlessness that is the consequence of original sin, and he prays that his God, offended by the sin, but loving his creation nevertheless, will raise him to life. A man may not respond with the gifts of remission of sin and eternal life; he may, however, exercise charity in imitation of God by raising a penitent through material means or by bestowing value or honor upon him. In effect, that is what Orgon does, and his charity in other circumstances would indeed be an example of good works. But everything about this gift—in the perspective of Orgon's desire to exercise godlike power and "charity," suggested by "vis-à-vis," and in the perspective of Tartuffe's blatant manipulation of him through public, excessive mortification directed toward him—everything about this gift seems improper, including Tartuffe's abased response: "C'est trop, me disait-il, c'est trop de la moitié, / Je ne mérite pas de vous faire pitié." Tartuffe denies he has any worth: "I do not deserve to arouse your pity."

These first words of his, recounted by Orgon, pose misleadingly the relationship, on which he plays, between the charitable source of power and the recipient of charity. The sinner's worthlessness, acknowledged in acts of mortification, is entirely overshadowed by God's love—charity—which is not a function of pity but a free gift. According to Christian ideology, *no one deserves* on the basis of merit to be saved. Mortification is a recognition of that doctrine; and it is not intended to arouse pity, either. Orgon does not extend alms to Tartuffe out of pity, compassion, or love; he gives because the self-mortifying Tartuffe has implicitly cast him in the role of the bountiful, charitable power. Orgon is invited, perversely, to play God and in the process, by good works and by the sacrament Tartuffe offers, to gain his own salvation.

Tartuffe's immediate distribution of the alms to the beggars at the church door repeats the sequence of mortification–charity. Tartuffe denies his worthiness, then gives charity, as if to provide a lesson— "à mes yeux," says Orgon—in charity from the most abject of penitents: the Christian gives away his possessions, which, according to New Testament teachings, are a stumbling block between man and salvation. In a sense, Tartuffe's is a greater deed of charity than Orgon's, since it occurs freely: the beggars are there, exposing their poverty but not proffering acts of mortification or instruments of sacramental activity to attract alms in a kind of unholy exchange like that to which Tartuffe tempts Orgon. But Tartuffe's charity and lesson soon enough prove instruments of exchange—for the power over Orgon's household that the first scene with Madame Pernelle suggests and for the material objects belonging to Orgon that Tartuffe has no intention of sharing with any beggar. Tartuffe is exchanging his situation as, literally, a "pauvre homme"—or, as Dorine calls him, a "gueux"—for one as the heir to Orgon's fortune. Orgon is deluded if he believes that "Enfin le Ciel chez moi me le fit retirer, / Et depuis ce temps-là tout semble y prospérer." On the contrary: his household is in complete disorder as it resists his attempts, with the support of Tartuffe, to subject children and wife to mortification that is far from Christian.

The opening scene and Orgon's dialogue with Dorine—the "pauvre homme" conversation—indicate that Orgon does not extend charity to his family. While imitating, in favoring Tartuffe, the archetypal relationship of a bountiful power to a being deprived of value, he violates the bonds linking a man to his natural dependents, which should also follow analogously the relationship of God and king to creation and subject and which should not be based on the mortifying assumption of his dependents' worthlessness. Orgon's interruption of Cléante's criticism establishes once and for all his perverse attitude to his family under Tartuffe's direction:

> Mon frère, vous seriez charmé de le connaître,
> Et vos ravissements ne prendraient point de fin.
> C'est un homme . . . qui, . . . ha! un homme . . . un homme enfin.
> Qui suit bien ses leçons goûte une paix profonde,
> Et comme du fumier regarde tout le monde.
> Oui, je deviens tout autre avec son entretien;
> Il m'enseigne à n'avoir affection pour rien,
> De toutes amitiés il détache mon âme;
> Et je verrais mourir frère, enfants, mère et femme,
> Que je m'en soucierais autant que de cela.
>
> (270–79)

Orgon cites Tartuffe's lessons as though they were gospel; in fact they are a misstatement of a passage from the Gospel of Matthew 10:37–39, where one is told to leave one's kin to follow Jesus. Orgon follows "un homme, enfin": not a divine being with a message of love, but a man who preaches human worthlessness—or worse. What Orgon expresses as dung, "fumier," might be more strongly stated on a stage less subject to niceties of language, and the unembellished thought with the perverse allusion to Matthew is offensive and un-Christian. Orgon considers his family, including the brother-in-law to whom he is speaking, deserving of neither love nor pity, as if they "ne méritaient pas de lui faire pitié," to paraphrase Tartuffe's words at the church door. The structural relationship binding a family in Christian charity is replaced by a detachment parodistically associated with an authoritative gospel and connected with an act of debasement: mortification is extended by Orgon to his family, even as he elevates himself to the ecstatic state of having "ravissements sans fin" and enjoying "une paix profonde." This attitude of detachment from people whom a husband and father should love ought not be confused with a Stoic ataraxia, with the detachment cherished by Montaigne as he explains it in the essay "On Solitude" (book 1, ch. 39), or with the attitude of Pascal. Sainte-Beuve's distinctions between the two French philosophers set them apart from

Orgon:

> Montaigne craignait de s'attacher aux autres, de peur d'avoir à en
> souffrir: Pascal craignait surtout qu'on ne s'attachât à lui, et de
> détourner ainsi les âmes de leur objet unique et de leur impérissable
> fin. Il y avait bien du zèle pour autrui sous cet appareil de froideur.
> On peut dire que le détachement de Pascal était porté sur un fond
> d'ardente charité et de compassion immense: celui de Montaigne ne
> reposait que sur un calcul de prudence et de bien-être.[2]

Orgon's detachment resembles nothing more than that of a demonic
power which takes pleasure in witnessing, even arranging, the humiliation of mankind through suffering and through reminders of
its imperfect and incurable body and nature. Such is the consequence
of following the gospel according to Tartuffe.

Tartuffe constructs his appeal to Elmire (iii, iii) on the same assumptions he proceeded upon with Orgon, casting himself in a
position of worthlessness—mortification—and assigning to her a
role associated with the power and charity of heaven. (Elmire, however, does not suffer from the psychological weaknesses of her husband.) The terms of his argument to seduce Elmire are established
in his greeting:

> Que le Ciel à jamais par sa toute bonté
> Et de l'âme et du corps vous donne la santé,
> Et bénisse vos jours autant que le désire
> Le plus humble de ceux que son amour inspire.

(879–82)

In his subsequent speeches, the attributes of heaven—"sa toute
bonté" capable of granting spiritual and physical health—are transferred to Elmire, while his mortification before heaven—"le plus
humble"—is repeated before her. Tartuffe confuses the power in
the face of which mortification is appropriate; his arguments distort
the proper functions of penitence. A perversity adheres to the conventional language of a suitor or seducer when it occurs in a context
of religious devotion like that set in Tartuffe's greeting.

2. Charles-Augustin de Sainte-Beuve, *Port-Royal*, Maxime Leroy, ed.,
Bibliothèque de la Pléiade (Paris: Gallimard, 1954), 2:306*n*.

During his declaration of passion in the speech beginning "L'amour qui nous attache aux beautés éternelles" (933–60), the movements indicated by the text also suggest his perversion, for it is probable that during the greeting he had knelt (before the crucifix, if one was on stage) to pray for Elmire's health: now he must kneel before Elmire herself. He repeats the vocabulary of heaven's powers and his own worthlessness:

Ce m'est, je le confesse, une audace bien grande
Que d'oser de ce coeur vous adresser l'offrande;
Mais j'attends en mes voeux tout de votre bonté,
Et rien des vains efforts de mon infirmité;
En vous est mon espoir, mon bien, ma quiétude,
De vous dépend ma peine ou ma béatitude,
Et je vais être enfin, par votre seul arrêt,
Heureux, si vous voulez, malheureux, s'il vous plaît.

(953–60)

But Tartuffe's insistence on his nullity and on Elmire's bounty recalls his emphases in his encounters with Orgon at church. After her brief objection, as the speech continues "Ah! pour être dévot, je n'en suis pas moins homme" (966), he dwells on that dichotomy in a conventional Petrarchist vocabulary to which the context lends the force of a perverse imitation of the relationship between a penitent and God:

Que si vous contemplez d'une âme un peu bénigne
Les tribulations de votre esclave indigne,
S'il faut que vos bontés veuillent me consoler
Et jusqu'à mon néant daignent se ravaler,
J'aurais toujours pour vous, ô suave merveille,
Une dévotion à nulle autre pareille.

(981–86)

Elmire responds to this language—and not to the subject Tartuffe introduces at the end of his speech, his discretion, on which he elaborates during fourteen verses ("Votre honneur avec moi ne court point de hasard . . . ," 987–1000).[3] She refers to "votre rhétorique

3. That Elmire ignores this subject may indicate that Molière added Tartuffe's lines on his discretion in order to complement the characterization

21

/ En termes assez forts" (1001–2), alluding to the vocabulary of omnipotence and worthlessness, the same notion that he again restates when he continues his declaration:

> Je sais que vous avez trop de bénignité,
> Et que vous ferez grâce à ma témérité,
> Que vous m'excuserez sur l'humaine faiblesse
> Des violents transports d'un amour qui vous blesse,
> Et considérerez, en regardant votre air,
> Que l'on n'est pas aveugle, et qu'un homme est de chair.
>
> (1007–12)

Tartuffe avers his frailty and nullity, and Elmire's quasi-divine attributes, at all three climaxes of his speech: at the first break, beginning at 953–60, when he kneels; at the second interruption, 981–86, when he again kneels, before the change in subject to discretion; and in conclusion, beginning at 1007.

When Damis suddenly springs from his hiding place, Tartuffe is still on his knees protesting a mortification that is hardly penitential. He remains in that position, silent, for sixty verses, 1013–73, while Damis and Elmire discuss him as though he were the nullity he has declared himself to be. In effect it seems that he is at the mercy of Elmire and Damis, who disagree over the matter of exercising power to condemn or spare him. The ultimate judge, Elmire realizes, is Orgon, who will refuse to believe any accusation of Tartuffe; she may also understand, as Tartuffe and the audience know from the paradigmatic behavior that occurred in church, that Orgon will raise in charity the mortified man, whose acts of penitence and self-accusation prove his saintliness. When the judge enters, Damis steps aside to reveal Tartuffe kneeling "là": ". . . je l'ai surpris là qui faisait à Madame / L'injurieux aveu d'une coupable

---

of Tartuffe as a religious hypocrite and a scoundrel, or to reduce the impact of Tartuffe's perverse use of the relationship between God and creature in his approach to Elmire. On the other hand, Elmire's failure to respond to the subject may also indicate that, even in the original banned version, Elmire distinguished between the underlying issue and a comparative diversion.

flamme" (III, v, 1061–62). Tartuffe in fact is in position to appeal to Orgon's desire to reward the penitent saint. He has only to address a speech of absolute self-mortification to stimulate Orgon's charity and his misplaced faith in the holiness of the confessing penitent: "Oui, mon frère, je suis un méchant, un coupable, / Un malheureux pécheur, tout plein d'iniquité, / Le plus grand scélérat qui jamais ait été . . ." (III, vi, 1074–86).

Elmire refused to respond to Tartuffe's bait, to exercise grace upon an undeserving creature; the strategy works with Orgon who may reenact the scene in church, again accepting the role of a powerful, charitable—godlike—figure who raises the saint from his mortification. Tartuffe once again is facing Orgon as though he were a representation of divinity, a crucifix upon an altar: "Tout le monde me prend pour un homme de bien; / Mais la vérité pure est que je ne vaux rien" (1099–1100). Tartuffe continues, remaining on his knees:

Accablez-moi de noms encor plus détestés:
Je n'y contredis point, je les ai mérités;
Et j'en veux à genoux souffrir l'ignominie,
Comme une honte due aux crimes de ma vie.

(1103–6)

Orgon begs Tartuffe to rise and may begin to lift him when he turns his attention to Damis: ". . . Mon frère, eh! levez-vous, de grâce! / (*À son fils*) Infâme" (1109–10).

But Tartuffe does not rise, interceding for Damis in a parody of the suffering servant: ". . . Laissez-le en paix. S'il faut, à deux genoux, / Vous demander sa grâce . . ." (1115–16). Tartuffe persists in this role. He grotesquely restrains Orgon from beating Damis at verse 1135. Orgon still curses his son: "Je te prive, pendard, de ma succession, / Et te donne de plus ma malédiction" (1139–40). Tartuffe's interceding behavior is an offensive parody of a virtuous, even Christlike figure, unjustly accused of sin, who defends his detractor. Now he virtually parodies words of Jesus: "O Ciel, pardonne-lui la douleur qu'il me donne!" (1142). He has been praying, however, not to heaven but to Orgon, who finally succeeds in raising him at

verse 1151: "Remettez-vous, mon frère, et ne vous fâchez pas."
"Remettez-vous" means both "recover" (in the sense of "calm down
and forget the sorrow Damis caused you") and "get up." Tartuffe
has been lifted from the compromising position before Elmire where
Damis had surprised him: he had remained on his knees for two
hundred lines. But once raised he declares that he will leave the
house in order to bring peace. This evidence of self-mortification
and renunciation arouses Orgon's charity to complete the model of
action established in the earlier speech to Cléante, and he names
Tartuffe his wife's guardian and the heir to his worldly goods: "Je
ne veux point avoir d'autre héritier que vous, / Et je vais de ce pas,
en fort bonne manière, / Vous faire de mon bien donation entière"
(1176–78). This gift is not alms Tartuffe will share with the poor,
but Orgon's entire fortune. To the limit of his worldly ability Orgon
imitates the bounty of a savior, raising and glorifying the abject
creature who in self-condemnation throws himself upon the mercy,
grace, and goodness of the God.

Tartuffe converts disaster to triumph by inducing Orgon to play
God. His mortification is a parodic, debasing imitation of a sacred
archetypal relationship between man and God. It is not difficult to
understand how such behavior might offend religious sensibilities,
and not only those of Molière's time. Anyone who takes seriously
the Christian ideology, or mythology, may be alienated by the spectacle of such blatant misrepresentation of the bond of divine compassion and love. The basis of comedy here is a deliberately distorted
version of holy things, specifically the relationship between man-
the-fallen-creature and God-the-forgiving-creator which provides an
article of faith or an assumption that supports and guarantees the
entire structure of Christian civilization. This perversion corresponds to Aristotle's description of comedy as representing *to
phaúlon*, the morally ugly or distorted. Tartuffe and Orgon act out
between themselves a morally repulsive version of an essential archetypal bond of great beauty from which man derives consolation
for his imperfections and hope for his future, and eternal, restoration
to his original uncorrupted state.

MORTIFICATION AND CHARITY IN *LE TARTUFFE*

That relationship between a bountiful, pardoning power and a creature who acknowledges his relative weakness (without, however, denying that he possesses some value as the creation of a God who saw that his creation was good and that man was very good) is reflected in the bonds between human figures of authority and their subjects. The king and the father exercise their authority upon subjects and children as though they were imitating as faithfully as possible the ideal or archetypal God–creation structure. A Christian father deals lovingly, mercifully, and justly with his family. Justly, because not to insist upon respect for standards of basic morals would encourage unethical, i.e., sinful behavior that leads to damnation, and to disorder in this life; mercifully, because human nature being what it is, the authority acknowledges the imperfection of his subjects. Christian love—charity—combines as a Pascalian "entre-deux" the space between the opposite poles of rigorous justice and flexible mercy.

Orgon, from the beginning, does not share in this "entre-deux." His dominant mode of exercising paternal authority is repression; that is established in the opening scene, even before he enters, through the dogmatic attitudes of his mother, Madame Pernelle, and the allusions to the rigorously puritanical controls over behavior inaugurated by Tartuffe. Toward Damis Orgon refuses to consider mercy, even at the behest of Tartuffe: his expulsion is swift. With Mariane in act II Orgon simply assumes her obedience and desire to please him; and she ignorantly, or blissfully, concurs, also assuming the goodness of her father and his knowledge of her love for her suitor, Valère. Her inability to defend her interests is a mark of her surprise: she is overwhelmed by her father's astounding, unexpected abuse of power. In effect, though, it belongs to the general pattern of the play. Her father's declared intention to marry her to Tartuffe imposes upon her a total mortification for which she is unprepared and which reduces her to the speechlessness of a creature whose value has been removed. The basis of Dorine's objection is that marriage of Mariane to a "gueux"—a man with no possessions, a man of no material worth—is to deny that she is

25

worthy of a man of parts, a gentleman whose accomplishments and manners indicate an inherent value. Mariane cannot believe that her father would so mortify her, and she cannot imagine herself married to and possessed by such a man: that is the ultimate mortification, the carnal joining of her youth, beauty, and innocence to all the repulsive attributes she must find in Tartuffe.

Orgon in effect humiliates his daughter in a perverse manner of mortification, for the act would destroy her innocence. She is not a great and proud sinner for whom penitence would provide a means of salvation. Dorine again makes the point: marriage to Tartuffe would make the young woman a sinner—she would quickly learn to cuckold her husband. Orgon's abuse of power and of Mariane's filial piety would not inspire acts of charity or Christian behavior.

Dorine's subsequent teasing of Mariane provides a parody of mortification. She graphically demonstrates what the marriage would reduce Mariane to, but at the same time she manages to turn the humiliation into a joke, acting out in a *numéro* of virtuoso farce a narrative of visits, carnival, the ape Fagotin, and even, with a pun intended on the girl's name, marionettes.

> Non, il faut qu'une fille obéisse à son père,
> Voulût-il lui donner un singe pour époux.
> Votre sort est fort beau: de quoi vous plaignez-vous?
> Vous irez par le coche en sa petite ville,
> Qu'en oncles et cousins vous trouverez fertile,
> Et vous vous plairez fort à les entretenir.
> D'abord chez le beau monde on vous fera venir;
> Vous irez visiter, pour votre bienvenue,
> Madame la baillive et Madame l'élue,
> Qui d'un siège pliant vous feront honorer.
> Là, dans le carnaval, vous pourrez espérer
> Le bal et la grand'bande, à savoir, deux musettes,
> Et parfois Fagotin et les marionettes,
> Si pourtant votre époux . . .

(II, iii, 654–67)

Instead of dying of humiliation, Mariane "dies of laughter": "Ah! tu me fais mourir," she says, adding, "De tes conseils plutôt songe

26

à me secourir" (667–68). Dorine returns, however, to the seriousness of Mariane's humiliation in another joke, a play on names that sums up the dilemma: ". . . vous serez, ma foi! Tartuffiée" (674).

When Valère enters, Mariane has been reduced to desperation, first by her father, then by Dorine: both subject her to forms of mortification, Orgon seriously, Dorine parodistically. It is no wonder that she responds so inappropriately to her suitor's questions concerning the rumored marriage. The *dépit amoureux* scene (II, iv), tedious and overdrawn as it is, reflects her desperate state. While with Dorine she had behaved helplessly, as though she had submitted entirely to Orgon's will and lost all her strength of character, Valère's interpretation of her situation in the worst possible light—he accuses her of complaisance—stings her pride. The quarrel brings out in the couple all the frailties to which lovers are subject: jealousy, suspicion, *amour-propre*. Acts of mortification are intended to condemn and provide penance for such human failings; but Orgon's mortification of his daughter ironically produces very different and perverse effects. Only Dorine seems to sense this. Valère certainly does not, for he behaves as uncharitably, as rigorously, and with as little sympathy for Mariane's humiliation as Orgon. Dorine finally reconciles the lovers in a benevolent act that permits each one to "save face"; that is, each is spared the humiliation of admitting error and neither is obliged to do penance. In effect the *dépit amoureux* is forgotten as Dorine encourages the lovers to cover it with an act of grace. That, however, does not solve the dilemma, although the graceful and free nature of their mutual pardon points the way to a solution. Mariane will beg grace of her father in act IV but will be further mortified by his refusal. Dorine's proposed strategies for putting off the marriage—feigning illness, evil omens, etc.—resemble those suggested by Valère and Frosine in *L'Avare* (which are forgotten as soon as they are brought up). They are dilatory measures that fail to strike at the heart of the problem and they are introduced but not put into effect. Stronger medicine is needed, Molière seems to be indicating, and expedients, clever though they may be, will not do.

Mariane's encounters with Orgon, Dorine, and Valère, while implicitly embracing essential sacred relationships, do not include specific verbal references to them; the action itself suffices to make an audience aware that Orgon is violating his bonds to his child and producing havoc, through her speechlessness, through Dorine's parody of mortification, finally through the outbreak of pride and stubbornness. In act IV, however, Molière explicitly has Mariane allude to sacred relationships and even reduces her to the position of a helpless suppliant, or mortified penitent, begging for mercy. Her speech contains the vocabulary of power and nullity characteristic of Tartuffe's earlier appeals to Elmire and Orgon.

> Mon père, au nom du Ciel, qui connaît ma douleur,
> Et par tout ce qui peut émouvoir votre coeur,
> Relâchez-vous un peu des droits de la naissance,
> Et dispensez mes voeux de cette obéissance;
> Ne me réduisez point par cette dure loi
> Jusqu'à me plaindre au Ciel de ce que je vous doi,
> Et cette vie, hélas! que vous m'avez donnée,
> Ne me la rendez pas, mon père, infortunée.
> Si, contre un doux espoir que j'avais pu former,
> Vous me défendez d'être à ce que j'ose aimer,
> Au moins, par vos bontés, qu'à vos genoux j'implore,
> Sauvez-moi du tourment d'être à ce que j'abhorre,
> Et ne me portez point à quelque désespoir,
> En vous servant sur moi de tout votre pouvoir.
>
> (IV, iii, 1279–92)

Molière places this prayer to a father in the context of sacred relationships with the appeal "au nom du Ciel," which here has greater force than it usually does in classical theater. Since the father-child relationship is isomorphic with that between God and man, or king and subject, the phrase "in the name of heaven" alludes to the clemency for which Christians hope. Mariane prays that Orgon act "par vos bontés" and take pity on her sorrows, not exercising his full powers as is his legal right. She both acknowledges her obligation to her father as her creator and implores him not to diminish her, not to make her deny the value of the life and the

relationship he bestowed on her. The appeal to mercy and grace—
to *générosité*—as opposed to legalistic obligation and contractual duty
refers to the nature of gifts freely granted without considerations of
self-interest: Orgon did not give her life, she assumes, to serve his
advantage. (But we suspect that his gifts to Tartuffe—alms, then
his fortune—are intended to serve his own interests as the bountiful
power, misconstrued as needing to promote its own advantage.) She
asks him in effect to imitate the sacred archetypal relationship as
properly understood; by acting nonlegalistically, according to the
promptings of the heart, giving freely without expectation of reward,
one does imitate the divinity, and by such imitation one demonstrates godliness and worth, giving God a reason, as it were, to
exercise grace and save humankind.

According to a rare explanation in the text, Orgon, "se sentant
attendrir," begins to feel charity in response to his daughter's prayers
and her mortification before him; but he dissuades himself:
"Allons, ferme, mon coeur, point de faiblesse humaine" (1293). It
is appropriate to imagine Molière starting to raise Mariane from her
knees, then catching himself in the saving act and dropping her, for
his Orgon here has the opportunity to yield in grace, like God, to
a penitent's prayer. His "faiblesse humaine" would in fact resemble
divine strength. In this context Mariane's preference for a cloister
over marriage to Tartuffe is also not the conventional device usually
found in comedy, for it recalls the bond between God and creation:
in the penitential "austérités" of the convent, the nuns trust exclusively in their God's grace and mercy to save them. But Orgon
dismisses that request of Mariane's as well; he commands her to rise
from her knees and paradoxically to reduce herself to nullity in a
marriage where she submits as a worthless creature of father and
husband: "Mortifiez vos sens avec ce mariage, / Et ne me rompez
pas la tête davantage" (1305–6).

Orgon immediately gets the treatment he deserves because he has
ignored the stirrings of charity and has chosen mortification for his
flesh and blood without clemency. His graceless act is like a hubristic
deed that summons forth a nemesis, and the audience is pleased that

his comeuppance arrives so promptly in a virtual peripeteia. Orgon spends 180 lines (as long as Tartuffe had remained kneeling in act III) under a table on all fours while Tartuffe demonstrates the very villainy he had earlier confessed. Molière makes Orgon resemble a man mortified and groveling on hands and knees while he witnesses his betrayer's callous, uncharitable, un-Christian behavior. Orgon is immediately diminished from his posture as a man before whom others knelt in prayer—as before a possible savior—to this humiliated position. That is where a perverse imitation of the sacred relationship has properly led him.

Tartuffe's situation also has changed. He no longer kneels before Elmire nor pretends worthlessness in order, by contrast, to cast Elmire as the source of bounties. He does use some of that vocabulary when he doubts her sincerity, but with significant shifts in meaning.

> Je puis croire ces mots un artifice honnête
> Pour m'obliger à rompre un hymen qui s'apprête;
> Et s'il faut librement m'expliquer avec vous,
> Je ne me fierai point à des propos si doux,
> Qu'un peu de vos faveurs, après quoi je soupire,
> Ne vienne m'assurer tout ce qu'ils m'ont pu dire,
> Et planter dans mon âme une constante foi
> Des charmantes bontés que vous avez pour moi.
>
> (IV, V, 1447–54)

"Bontés" are now explicitly sexual favors. In his next speech Tartuffe weakly alludes to the nullity on which he had previously insisted:

> Moins on mérite un bien, moins on l'ose espérer.
> Nos voeux sur des discours ont peine à s'assurer.
> On soupçonne aisément un sort tout plein de gloire,
> Et l'on veut en jouir avant que de le croire.
> Pour moi, qui crois si peu mériter vos bontés,
> Je doute du bonheur de mes témérités;
> Et je ne croirai rien, que vous n'ayez, Madame,
> Par des réalités su convaincre ma flamme.
>
> (1459–66)

Tartuffe uses "on" to generalize; this devalues the vocabulary to

30

conventional rhetoric. The sacred relationship, according to which a divine source of power extends charity to a creature in mortification, that is perversely imitated in the comedy is now diminished to a series of empty words—a completely appropriate reduction since Tartuffe does not believe in the sacred relationship which he manipulates for selfish ends: that is what makes him a hypocrite. The "doubting Thomas" attitude he expresses, his pretended lack of hope, also indicates that he no longer follows the strategy of imitating, albeit perversely, the sacred relationship: the Christian living in faith and hope does not demand proofs of his salvation.

Orgon meanwhile remains a speechless witness of his own humiliation, like Mariane in act II. When at last he emerges (as Damis emerged in act III: it seems as though Molière has given Orgon in this passage the significant postures and gestures of his children and Tartuffe earlier in the play) to denounce Tartuffe and banish him (as he had disinherited Damis: Orgon repeats his own action), he finds that it is too late. He had exercised the power of charity by raising Tartuffe from mortification in act III and giving him the house, but Tartuffe is not about to reciprocate the gesture. Declaring himself heaven's champion, he does not imitate God by forgiveness and restoration. Act IV ends as Tartuffe abuses the sacred values that Orgon chose to ignore or abuse when Mariane had invoked them as the basic structure of the family.

In act V Tartuffe's perverse imitation of sacred relationships extends to the bonds between subject and king. The structure of this act in effect, although not in appearance, recapitulates the model of the preceding acts: Orgon, with his household, has been reduced literally—not figuratively—to worthlessness, humiliated and humbled; he does not expect any saving power to raise him, least of all a prince against whom he committed a criminal offense by harboring the compromising documents of a friend who opposed the sovereign in civil rebellion. Orgon, however, is rescued against all hope (or against all despair) in a stunning act of clemency toward him and of justice toward Tartuffe by that prince, offended and forgiving. (The prince in effect occupies another Pascalian "entre-deux" between opposing extremes.) This salvation and this justice are genuine and authoritative, not perverse, representations of divine archetypes.

In appearance the fifth act is constructed much like the last act of *Dom Juan*, produced in 1665 as the next play Molière composed after the first, banned version of *Tartuffe*. It consists of a series of visits to the threatened household by Damis, Madame Pernelle, Monsieur Loyal, Valère, and Tartuffe and l'Exempt, the royal officer. (Dom Juan also extends his perverse imitation of sacred relationships to a higher level in act V, directly challenging God, as it were, by religious hypocrisy—by becoming a Tartuffe.) Damis and Valère propose ways to save Orgon, Damis by characteristically championing violence (1634–37), Valère by offering money and a carriage in which to flee Paris. Neither of these solutions, however, would resolve the dilemma. Monsieur Loyal and Tartuffe with the officer threaten Orgon. These visits introduce a rhythm of despair, inadequate solution, despair, a solution—still inadequate but temporarily expedient—and despair. They also engender a rhythm of reconciliation, between father and son, between father and suitor (and, hence, between father and daughter), alternating with discord, in the visits of Madame Pernelle, Monsieur Loyal, and Tartuffe. The king's pardon, following the apparent threat personified in his officer, provides an ultimate salvation and reconciliation that joins the two rhythmic structures of the act. (The king also commits a mortified Tartuffe to prison, thus ironically fulfilling the intention declared by Tartuffe in his first speech.)

The sovereign discerns in Tartuffe's accusation an attempt to pervert the bond linking subject and king. By pardoning Orgon he restores the relationship operative between king and subject, God and creation, absolute power and relative—only relative—nullity that had been perversely imitated throughout the play. Charity is exercised to rescue the subject from his mortification: the penitent is restored to dignity and enabled once again to function—as a man with inherent value—in relationships no longer distorted by perverse interpretations of Christian ideology.

In denouncing Orgon Tartuffe had cited the prince's interest as his main motive. He takes the king's name in vain:

> . . . l'intérêt du Prince est mon premier devoir;
> De ce devoir sacré la juste violence
> Étouffe dans mon coeur toute reconnaissance,
> Et je sacrifierais à de si puissants noeuds
> Ami, femme, parents, et moi-même avec eux.
>
> (v, vii, 1880–84)

This statement recalls Orgon's in act I, that Tartuffe

> . . . m'enseigne à n'avoir affection pour rien,
> De toutes amitiés il détache mon âme;
> Et je verrais mourir frère, enfants, mère et femme,
> Que je m'en soucierais autant que de cela.
>
> (275–79)

Cléante had responded to Orgon's protestation: "Les sentiments humains, mon frère, que voilà!" Elmire and Dorine comment in similar fashion on Tartuffe's declaration:

> EL.: L'imposteur!
> DOR.: Comme il sait, de traîtresse manière,
> Se faire un beau manteau de tout ce qu'on révère!
>
> (1885–86)

The sacred relationships—"tout ce qu'on révère"—are distorted, but not only by Tartuffe. Orgon, mortified, then saved, still misses the point as he had in act IV with Mariane; he remains comically uncomprehending of the mystery of charity that is being enacted upon him. Only at the very end, after Cléante has provided a clue, does Orgon convert to unsullied values and cease to be a comic figure.

In the last scene Orgon's misuse of basic sacred values is emphasized before it is annulled in the concluding lines of the play. He reproaches Tartuffe the betrayal of his charity: "Mais t'es-tu souvenu que ma main charitable, / Ingrat, t'a retiré d'un état misérable?" (1877–78). Gifts are not charity, however, when their motive is not love of man or God, but self-interest. Orgon's charity allowed him to imitate the bountiful power, but without love. Tartuffe exploited this confused desire, which was not necessarily limited to Orgon, for the syndrome is to be found amongst members of the audience, who witness a representation of their attitudes and behavior too. Orgon acts on an impulse arising from a view of human nature inspired by the Christian mythology of the Fall: to purchase salvation with material means at his disposal and to imitate God and king, expecting those to whom "charity" is extended to acknowledge, in their gratitude and obligation, the essential gap separating himself as giver from themselves as objects of "charity."

Such an assumption conceals an abysmal flaw. The gap between any two men is not essential but accidental; birth and chance separate fortunate from wretched. Molière's Epicureanism feeds his humanistic Christianity. The gap between men differs in kind from that between God-the-creator-and-savior and his creation, and, according to the dominant political ideology of Molière's period, from that between king and subject. These distinctions may recall Pascal's definition of three orders. He emphasizes the enormous—the infinite—difference separating the two highest orders, those of spirit (*esprit:* spirit—or mind, intelligence) and of charity. For Pascal, that infinite gap might produce a vertiginous feeling of impotence; on the other hand, man can hope to attain to the second order, and by his capacity for thought he can obtain some specific dignity appropriate to his own order. Man is not a nullity for Pascal, or for Molière. The separation in essence between God and creature—that space in the great chain of being between God and the angels—or between king and subject may create the impression of man's relative nullity before the infinite power and goodness of God and king. In absolute terms, however, no creature is without some value; no being is deprived entirely of the worth with which the creator endowed him. And at the opposite pole, no man may be the all or the infinite power that is divinity: a man who properly imitates the bountiful power vis-à-vis other men cannot benefit or suffer from the impression of all versus nothing, for the gap between a human agent of charity and a human recipient of charity cannot ever resemble that between God and man. The aim of charity—the imitation of divine grace—is to become ethically like the divinity, to diminish the gap in essence between God and man: although this is an impossible wish, good works do allow man in a metaphoric sense to realize his ethical likeness to God. Orgon and Tartuffe may regard family, friends, and benefactors as no better than a pile of dung. But Molière's king, like his God, does not. The sovereign recognizes and rewards deeds of merit committed by his subjects that reflect the value they possess by nature and education, inheritance and practice. He opposes the pessimistic, antihumanistic position exploited by Tartuffe in his behavior in church and in the scenes of mortification before Elmire and Orgon. Orgon's humiliation on all fours suggests that through Tartuffe's influence he has lost human values natural to man and, in a religiously oriented social context, seen as God's purpose in creation: the recurrent refrain in the opening chapter of Genesis is, after all, "And God saw that it [what had been created] was good"; the refrain following the creation of man becomes "And God saw that it was very good." Tartuffe and Orgon would deny the underlying ethical value of the creation and the judgment of God. And, playing God, Orgon becomes a beast on all fours, crawling, as it were, like the serpent condemned for perverting original innocence in paradise.

The ultimate point made by the king's officer is that the sovereign pardons, and that the subject deserves to be forgiven because of actions indicating his essential value.

Oui, de tous vos papiers, dont il [Tartuffe] se dit le maître,
Il [the king] veut qu'entre vos mains je dépouille le traître.
D'un souverain pouvoir, il brise les liens
Du contrat qui lui fait un don de tous vos biens,
Et vous pardonne enfin cette offense secrète
Où vous a d'un ami fait tomber la retraite;
Et c'est le prix qu'il donne au zèle qu'autrefois
On vous vit témoigner en appuyant ses droits,
Pour montrer que son coeur sait, quand moins on y pense,
D'une bonne action verser la récompense,
Que jamais le mérite avec lui ne perd rien,
Et que mieux que du mal il se souvient du bien.

(1933–44)

This position negates the attitude exploited by Tartuffe. Orgon attracts the king's grace and free pardon through good works that the king remembers—that are, as it were, always present in the mind of the authoritative and all-knowing power. The king does not have to justify his acts; the insistence on Orgon's merits suggests, however, that despite his corruption man retains value—the godlike qualities are not eradicated—and he remains capable, when touched by grace and converted, of again exercising those virtues in action.

The comedy's final subject is Orgon's conversion to proper Christian values in imitation of the prince, who acted in imitation of heaven as the Christian hopes that heaven will act toward him. Orgon must not recriminate against Tartuffe, for whom conversion is also hoped. The last speeches indicate that in response to the king's bounty, man must imitate the Idea of Goodness in his own deeds. The king as paradigm provides the exemplum of action. Man follows suit, not to deserve salvation, which remains a mystery, but to assure the human values and civilization that the mythology embodies. We sanctify human values by imitating in our actions the Idea of the Good, when we act out properly the structural relationships operative amongst men in a hierarchical society and between man and God in Nature. When we imitate those structures perversely, we destroy human values and we are ludicrous: we are figures of comedy, inferior and morally perverse.

Orgon needs to be reminded of this notion by Cléante when he abuses Tartuffe:

Or.: Hé bien! te voilà, traître . . .
Cl.:   Ah! mon frère, arrêtez,
     Et ne descendez point à des indignités;
     À son mauvais destin laissez un misérable,
     Et ne vous joignez point au remords qui l'accable:
     Souhaitez bien plutôt que son coeur en ce jour
     Au sein de la vertu fasse un heureux retour,
     Qu'il corrige sa vie en détestant son vice
     Et puisse du grand Prince adoucir la justice . . .

                                         (1947–54)

As for Orgon, ". . . à sa bonté vous irez à genoux / Rendre ce que demande un traitement si doux" (1955–56). The rhyme "genoux"/ "doux" repeats in reverse order the rhyme with which Tartuffe entered church in Orgon's narrative. Cléante's advice, with its echo of Tartuffe's abject mortification, evokes the image of Orgon kneeling before the charitable power that has rescued him, not in mortification but in grateful submission and acknowledgment of the essential gap between them. Orgon may also hope, with some confidence, that the king will gracefully raise him and enable him to imitate properly, vis-à-vis—with respect to—his own family and all other subjects, the values, or the idea, of which the gesture of raising from penitence is the sign. Orgon's last speech acknowledges his obligations toward the king and then indicates that he will imitate the king in a grace-filled and generous action toward Valère, who has proven his nobility:

> Oui, c'est bien dit: allons à ses pieds avec joie
> Nous louer des bontés que son coeur nous déploie.
> Puis, acquittés un peu

—and "un peu" denotes that the obligation is infinite and can never be satisfied—

> de ce premier devoir,
> Aux justes soins d'un autre il nous faudra pourvoir,
> Et par un doux hymen couronner en Valère
> La flamme d'un amant généreux et sincère.
>
> (1957–62)

The play concludes with allusions to marriage, like most traditional comedy, following the ritual unions of Aristophanic Old Comedy and the conventional happy endings of Roman comedy based on Menander and New Comedy. Marriage occurs before an altar where a man and a woman, kneeling in all humility before God and "vis-à-vis"—next to—each other, in mutual recognition of their intrinsic value, commit themselves to imitate God's bond of grace to his creation. These rituals acknowledge and imitate properly the sacred relationship between God and man, between all the analogues

37

of God and man upon which rest the values of civilization for which the Judeo-Christian mythology is the *sine qua non*. Tartuffe is the enemy from within of that civilization, who, as he abuses and perversely, offensively, imitates the sacred relationship, appeals to that corrupt, envious part of human nature in Orgon—and in the offended, denying, self-righteous, virtuous spectator, "mon semblable, mon frère"—which always strives to oppose the natural order and to be not man, mistakenly scorned as a valueless nullity, but, in a manner misconceived, unloving and unbountiful, the divinity.

· 2 ·

OBLIGATION IN
DOM JUAN

Dom Juan, composed in the shadow of the banned *Tartuffe*, is a machine-play, a "spectacular" in the etymological sense, whose use of mechanical devices in the tomb and the Statue belongs to a pattern of gestures implicit in the text which shape the comedy's structure and meaning. Sganarelle's gestures during his opening speech supplement his praise of snuff. Like the allusions to kneeling in *Tartuffe*, they are recalled throughout the play and, in an entirely different sense, in his final speech as he cries for his wages. Molière, playing the role in 1665, must have brought the full tradition of comic turns and pranks, inflection and gesture of the Italian commedia to his delivery. But seventeen years had passed and Molière was dead when the play was first printed by La Grange, who, acting Dom Juan, may never have seen Sganarelle's gestures at the play's beginning or end. He was offstage, probably preparing to enter; and by 1682 memory of Molière's gestures during rehearsals would have dimmed. Even if the edition were based on Molière's own script, no detailed gestural directions would appear, since the author-director would need no written reminders. Besides, stage directions are rare enough in classical plays, and must be inferred from the speeches. La Grange included a few obvious indications: holding a snuffbox, falling down, and so on. The text must furnish other gestures as Molière might have directed: performance style, always

This chapter appeared in somewhat different form in *Romanic Review* (1974), 45:175–200. Reprinted by permission.

a question of varying declamation and movement, reflects the text most closely when the playwright participates in the staging and realizes auctorial intentions.

When the curtains part, Sganarelle holds a snuffbox as an instrument for challenging the authority of Aristotle and philosophy on the subject of ethics. His mock-serious attitude jars with the patent absurdity of his statement, particularly in the mid-seventeenth century when snuff was considered a doubtful substance, a vice rather than a source of virtue.

> Quoi que puisse dire Aristote et toute la Philosophie, il n'est rien d'égal au tabac: c'est la passion des honnêtes gens, et qui vit sans tabac n'est pas digne de vivre. Non-seulement il réjouit et purge les cerveaux humains, mais encore il instruit les âmes à la vertu, et l'on apprend avec lui à devenir honnête homme.

The surprising juxtaposition of Aristotle and snuff provokes laughter: Aristotle said nothing about tobacco, which entered Europe as a result of Renaissance voyages of discovery in the New World. The declaration that life without snuff is not worthy of humans exemplifies Sganarelle's ridiculous reasoning, accompanied by pedantic gesture: the forefinger raised, the eyes staring at the snuffbox. This section may even be punctuated by a sneeze if Sganarelle takes snuff at this moment. (If he sampled it before the curtains opened, he may have sneezed before beginning the panegyric, in a startling opening gesture.) The sneeze marks the absurd assertion linking snuff and virtue: a gesture shows the foolishness of Sganarelle's claim that snuff is indispensable to virtue, the ethical and happy life which is sought by Aristotle in the *Nicomachean Ethics* and which is the principal aim of philosophy.

Sganarelle then develops the notion that snuff affects the *honnête homme* in society:

> Ne voyez-vous pas bien, dès qu'on en prend, de quelle manière obligeante on en use avec tout le monde, et comme on est ravi d'en donner à droit et à gauche, partout où l'on se trouve? On n'attend pas même qu'on en demande, et l'on court au-devant du souhait des gens: tant

il est vrai que le tabac inspire des sentiments d'honneur et de vertu à tous ceux qui en prennent.

He offers snuff to people imagined all over the stage and to Gusman. This polite gesture has ramifications beyond social amenities, according to Sganarelle, for he would persuade Gusman that snuff leads to the good life. Sganarelle poses as a benefactor who does not wait to be asked for a gift of inestimable value if it miraculously confers honor and virtue. Were snuff such a wonder drug, Gusman would owe his bliss to Sganarelle. Could he ever adequately express his gratitude, or free himself of the debt with some commensurate action? Molière did not lightly choose his words as Sganarelle describes the "manière obligeante" of offering snuff by people "ravi" to pass it around. "Obliging," derived from *ob-ligare*, means "binding to," usually through service or favor; even the relatively rare "much obliged" still contains the notion of debt implied as an expression of gratitude. Sganarelle's civil gesture, performing the most valuable service, would place Gusman in his infinite debt; and while he should delight in conferring virtue upon Gusman, he is "ravi" because Gusman, unable to repay the obligation, must, as a virtuous man, acknowledge Sganarelle as the source of his happiness. Through Sganarelle, whose ridiculous speech and movements provoke laughter, Molière parodies civil gesture to raise the serious question of the dynamics of egoism underlying the practices of *honnêteté*.

The encomium of snuff introduces Dom Juan's fundamental dilemma concerning the "dialectic of obligation": how to remain free of debts not easily reckoned in measurable, and consequently commensurable, terms; how to shun obligations that reduce him to infinite debtor status; and how to appear the boundless creditor of people to whom in fact he owes much. Dom Juan, Sganarelle, and most other characters expect a person performing a service or favor to enjoy an ethical advantage. The recipient is indebted to the benefactor until a commensurate service, rendered in payment, cancels the original debt. Most relationships among men occur within such a dialectic of obligation, and the favors are answerable: few services are infinite in worth. An offer of snuff, without the ultimate value Sganarelle attributes to it, typifies the polite gesture that creates a "social obligation," usually taken as a matter of course, and with a pinch of salt, in *honnête* circles. According to one point of view, however, Pascal's, La Rochefoucauld's, and Hobbes', civil gestures actually disguise the gentleman's self-interest, his *amour-propre*, his instinct to tyrannize by creating relationships of master–slave between himself as benefactor and his social peers. "Chaque moi est l'ennemi et voudrait être le tyran des autres" (Pensée 455 in Brunschvicg's standard numbering), even in polite society where conventional gesture establishes an appearance of civility without changing the fundamental nature of man, which breaks out in moments of stress and challenge.[1] Generous gestures are seen to spring from egoistic motives; mutually reciprocal "obliging" gestures sublimate the desire for irreversibly obligating acts. The dialectic of obligation is a version of Hegel's master–slave dialectic.

The basic ethical structure of *Dom Juan* concerns the debtor's response to his awareness of debt, particularly when life-and-death is at stake. That is rarely the case in comedy, or in real life; but in this play, after act I, it is a question of life-and-death at every moment. The play's larger content, which is the point of contact between the comedy and reality, concerns the basic relationship of life-and-death between God and man: the initial giving of life and, in a Christian framework, the remission of sins and the eternal salvation of the soul. Those gifts lie outside the dialectic of obligation, for reasons to be discussed in the context of the great scene of the Poor Man (III, ii). Dom Juan invents debts to himself to reverse relationships with creditors; he follows the strategy of a self-interested creditor to exaggerate his services and paralyze his debtor. But Dom Juan fails, trapped by situations of enormous debt and reduced to a paralyzed slave.

1. Jan Miel has a pertinent discussion of this point in his *Pascal and Theology* (Baltimore: The Johns Hopkins University Press, 1969), pp. 170–71.

The final gesture in Sganarelle's praise of snuff epitomizes the strategy of reversing debtor relationships. "Mais c'est assez de cette matière. Reprenons un peu notre discours," he says, as transition to the subject of Elvire's pursuit of Dom Juan. *Matière* means both "subject" and "stuff": "enough of that subject (snuff)" and "enough of that material (snuff)." The double meaning indicates that Sganarelle relinquishes the snuffbox to Gusman; it does not reappear in the play because it belongs to Gusman, a character whose language marks him as closer than Sganarelle to elegant circles where snuffboxes are found. Sganarelle covers his embarrassment with the pun on *matière*. Gusman's gestural claim to the snuffbox startlingly provokes the intuition that Sganarelle played benefactor with Gusman's own snuff. Gusman must have offered a pinch before the curtains parted. Did Sganarelle intend the praise of snuff to distract from a simple social obligation while using Gusman's snuffbox to annul the obligation and create a debt of virtue and happiness toward himself by Gusman? That would summarize the pattern of Dom Juan's actions: attempts to cancel or distract from real obligations and embarrassments, while making creditors appear indebted to him. The snuff-speech provides a paradigm for later episodes, exaggerated to absurdity in words and gestures that partially veil its significance. The pun of the transition acts like a shock, making the audience quickly reconsider the praise of snuff and accompanying gestures, while it laughs at Sganarelle, forced to return the snuffbox to its owner: snuff has produced no virtue in this would-be pilferer.

Although Sganarelle fails to become Gusman's benefactor, he proceeds to establish superiority in judgment over Gusman and in ethics over Dom Juan through criticism of his master. Sganarelle again plays Gusman's benefactor with his character analysis, as he later acts the part with the peasants in act II, giving similar derogatory information about Dom Juan to elicit their gratitude. Some of his pleasure lingers when Dom Juan enters (I, ii): he answers Dom Juan casually, challenges Dom Juan's behavior, and wisecracks that he had not mentioned Elvire's presence because, "Monsieur, vous ne me l'avez pas demandé." He apparently feels no obligation to volunteer significant information! Dom Juan's own good mood shows in his eager account of constant infidelities, which develops Sganarelle's observation that Dom Juan "se plaît à se promener de liens en liens, et n'aime guère demeurer en place." Along with movement and change, those baroque categories, Molière stresses the breaking of bonds, *liens*, derived also from *ligare*. Dom Juan resembles a purveyor of snuff, who offers love to beauties all around him, creating obligations toward himself, and feeling no bonds toward the women chosen for seduction. After all, he is giving, they are taking.

He plays on the idea of engagement, a form of obligation: *gages*—wages—are pledges of good faith, and he introduces a more general obligation, dictated by nature, the only one he respects because it permits him to ignore the civil and legal obligations implied by marriage. "J'ai beau être engagé, l'amour que j'ai pour une belle n'engage point mon âme à faire injustice aux autres; je conserve des yeux pour voir le mérite de toutes, et rends à chacune les hommages et les tributs où la nature nous oblige." The speech leads to a comparison with Alexander the Great, wishing for new worlds, and with conquerors who cannot "se résoudre à borner leurs souhaits": "je me sens un coeur à aimer toute la terre," he exclaims. The image of a limitless conqueror is revealing in the light of the dialectic of obligation, for Alexander could leave conquests because it was in the nature of things that he move on without restriction from one place to another in order to satisfy his destiny. He operated on a level where ordinary obligations did not obtain. He owed nothing, while all was owed to him.

Sganarelle correctly perceives that Dom Juan talks like a book. Dom Juan follows the Petrarchist-précieux conceit of woman as a fortified place to be captured; and Alexander, in Molière's period, represented a type of romantic hero for whom women would abandon their virtue with no thought for tomorrows. (Alexander, of course, came to be a figure for Louis XIV as well.) But Sganarelle's remark suggests that happens only in fiction, while in reality women expect to be courted and wed within the dialectic of obligation. Dom

Juan is not free, after all, to love "toute la terre," but is limited to a finite number of conventional women.

Molière does not delay in confronting Dom Juan with the most recent woman, whose presence creates an embarrassment Alexander never knew. Elvire comes to recall her husband to the bonds of marriage. Dom Juan's euphoria, culminating in the comparison with Alexander, is interrupted, and he shifts the burden of her vexation to Sganarelle who, also embarrassed, explains his and Dom Juan's departure with a reference to the comparison, now odious to Dom Juan because Elvire has proved it inaccurate. Molière allows Dom Juan a chance to seize the ethical advantage, however, after Elvire's enumeration of a courtier's conventional defenses; his response draws on what she should have argued: obligations to heaven, vows and pledges broken to marry him. He pretends to be her benefactor, instead of the faithless moral pauper he is. Like Sganarelle with the snuffbox, he borrows arguments Elvire had at her disposal and uses them hypocritically against her to establish her ethical inferiority.

Characteristically, he ignores her final imprecations and, after a pause for reflection, a strange stage direction for silent gesture, he goes off, his euphoria dampened but already on the upswing through his posture as Elvire's ethical superior and benefactor, and through his eagerness to break the bonds between a young couple whose happiness has aroused his desire.

In act I, obligations are engendered by: snuff, which creates a social obligation, an infinite one if snuff were really a means to a virtuous and happy life; and marriage, which creates legal and heaven-sanctioned obligations. Self-styled benefactors, Sganarelle and Dom Juan, behave exclusively for reasons of self-interest. In the remainder of the play, benefactors give life, and Dom Juan's relationships occur in a context of life-and-death. The stakes are increased infinitely; unlike those associated with snuff, they are real and everlasting. Dom Juan persists in mocking these terms with civil gestures meant to distract from the overwhelming debt of life he incurs, and to make him seem a creditor-benefactor instead of an infinite debtor. If his subterfuges are perceived as brilliant esthetic gestures, the point is missed, and Dom Juan cannot be appreciated as a comic creation. For the gestures do not hide the fact that no polite motion can countervail the gift of life. The crucial question, though, that Dom Juan's displays of virtuosity sidestep, is whether any recompense at all is required to offset this gift: is the gift of life contained within the dialectic of obligation?

Life-and-death may seem too serious a topic for a genre that usually excludes death. A protagonist may be laughed off the stage, but is not punished with death for errors and misdeeds. Dom Juan is exceptional, for death is ultimately the wages of his sin: his life is the pledge forfeited for breaking faith. Death, however, does not simply occur as a miraculous intervention to destroy Dom Juan, or as an opportunity to exploit machines on stage. The shadow of death is cast more and more deeply across the play from act II onwards; in act III the theme of life-and-death recurs in each episode; and the appearances of the Statue in subsequent acts are like visitations of Death personified.

When act II begins, Dom Juan has been saved from death by Pierrot. Against this background, the act's single episode exhibits Dom Juan's frustration and embarrassment when confronted by two peasant girls to whom he has promised marriage. A situation he has made turns against him. This reversal is typical of Molière's comic dramaturgy in other plays (for example, *L'École des femmes* and *Les Femmes savantes*), and it is repeated in act III. But the ethical point supported by this basic comic action deals with a greater theme, the great lord's treatment of the benefactor who has saved his life. Pierrot's narrative of the rescue provides a context for the act, as Sganarelle's praise of snuff sets the context for Dom Juan in act I. Molière again uses gesture to bolster the text, even extending gesture to the language itself: the patois establishes character and makes the audience perceive that Dom Juan is beholden to a bumpkin. Pierrot intends his narrative to impress Charlotte, his fiancée, and consequently, while acting out the account, he stresses his own qualities of keen eyesight and shrewdness in persuading Lucas to bet against him on a sure thing. (A bet, incidentally, is another form of pledged obligation.) Molière emphasizes Pierrot's lack of specific moral worth: he is immodest, self-interested (he collected the bet from Lucas before setting out to the rescue), and more taken with the profit from his wager than with having saved a life. All that detracts not a whit from the fact that the great lord's life depends on him.

Pierrot is also bound to the dialectic of obligation, not with Dom Juan, however, from whom he asks no reward, but with Charlotte. His possessiveness shows in a demand that she respond to his attentions, as gifts and serenades obligate her to. Dom Juan's attempt to seduce Charlotte betrays his benefactor, who sets great store, in his engagement to Charlotte, on the dialectic of obligation reduced to the absurd level of serenades, tokens, and love-pinches. Dom Juan at no time mentions his debt to Pierrot. Worse, on learning of Charlotte's engagement, he courts her more ardently: "Quoi? une personne comme vous serait la femme d'un simple paysan! Non, non, c'est profaner tant de beautés . . ." He strikes Pierrot when the peasant claims his rights, but grows silent when Pierrot recalls the rescue: ". . . ça n'est pas bian de battre les gens, et ce n'est pas la récompense de v's avoir sauvé d'être nayé." Dom Juan threatens Pierrot again only after Pierrot regrets having saved him, as if the remark nullified Dom Juan's debt: "Si j'avais su ça tantôt, je me serais bien gardé de le tirer de gliau, et je gli aurais baillé un bon coup d'aviron sur la tête." Dom Juan reacts viciously when he feels himself quit of obligation by the expressed wish that he had been knocked underwater by Pierrot's oar. This manipulation of the dialectic of obligation is specious, for the fact of the rescue remains. Dom Juan seizes an opportunity to escape the debt easily, and to pose as Charlotte's benefactor.

Charlotte and Sganarelle also pose as benefactors, with regard to Pierrot. Charlotte tries to convert her broken engagement into a service: "Va, va, Pierrot, ne te mets point en peine: si je sis Madame, je te ferai gagner queuque chose, et tu apporteras du beurre et du fromage cheux nous." Playing the grande dame, the embarrassed obligee caught in the act imitates Dom Juan to appear the benefactor.

She abjures the unmeasurable ethical values implicit in betrothal, and invents material values owed her. Sganarelle also pretends to serve Pierrot, and is struck for his pains. He intervenes to obligate Dom Juan's victims to himself; that is why he denounces his master, out of earshot, at the end of the act. But the debts do not take shape, as Dom Juan's slap and return make Sganarelle abandon his poses of philanthropy. His apparent pity for Pierrot turns into "peste soit du maroufle," while he must swallow Dom Juan's taunt, "Te voilà payé de ta charité." But charity the gesture cannot be, if a self-interested Sganarelle wants superiority and obligation. Such self-seeking is typical of all the characters in this act, none of whom respects ethical obligations and performs services disinterestedly. Pierrot comes closest to performing a service freely by saving Dom Juan; its selflessness is mitigated, however, by his insistence on the wager.

But Dom Juan's debt to Pierrot differs in nature from all the other obligations, actual and desired. Betrothal and the protection of victims seem pale next to the debt of life itself. The stakes of bene-factor–obligee relationships are increased to that level in act III, where every episode involves life-and-death. While Dom Juan re-fuses in act II to acknowledge his debt of life to a peasant, from act III on he is disconcerted by the thought of owing his life to nearly every character introduced, from the hermit to the Statue. He is caught by the consequences of construing his debts, great and small, in terms of the dialectic of obligation. That attitude must now be examined, before we look at the events of act III, particularly the scene with the Poor Man.

Within the dialectic of obligation, a benefactor remains superior until the recipient of a service has rendered an equivalent one. Cer-tain acts of great magnitude, however, produce unrepayable debts. The value implicit in giving or saving life, bestowing a great fortune, or raising to a rank of undeserved merit cannot easily be matched in equivalent action, because the benefactor will probably never be in need of such action. That creates a problem, for although people generally consider great gifts desirable, they are uncomfortable with the consciousness of debt such gifts induce. As Pascal noted, "trop de bienfaits irritent" (Pensée 72).

But immeasurable services do not properly belong to a dialectic of obligation, a movement back and forth between parties who hold a measurable, temporary ethical advantage: a pinch of snuff can be offered to the original purveyor, and it confers no boundless ethical values of virtue and happiness, Sganarelle to the contrary. Acts like saving life do not originate in a desire for moral slaves, but in grace and charity. (The whole question of *générosité* in Corneille is at issue here, incidentally.) A gap exists between common and commensurable action within the dialectic of obligation and acts of charity: in seventeenth-century terms it is an abyss. Pierrot did not save Dom Juan to alter or establish dynamics of power between himself as creditor and the nobleman as debtor. He seeks no reward, and does not speak as though Dom Juan were immeasurably beholden to him. He mentions a "récompense" strictly in reaction to Dom Juan's treachery. The peasant's behavior stands as an object lesson to the man saved, and to the audience, of an act of charity; and this point is strengthened by Molière's insistence on Pierrot's toeing the line on the dialectic of obligation where his fiancée is involved, and by Pierrot's relegation of importance to the keenness of his eyesight rather than to the actual rescue. Dom Juan acts ungratefully, feeling overwhelmingly burdened with a debt of life to Pierrot. He is comic not only because the situations he manipulates entrap and embarrass him, but especially because he is caught by the dialectic of obligation where it does not apply: he misinterprets a fundamental relationship of charity as equivalent to Sganarelle's pinch of snuff, a civil gesture that the valet claims to confer immeasurable, unpayable values and correspondingly large debts; he cannot imagine acts of grace committed without expectation or desire of reward or obligation. And this misconception demeans and reduces the sublime, the saving of life, to the ridiculous and the vicious, the pushing of snuff à la Sganarelle. The scenes with the Poor Man in act III and with Dom Louis and Done Elvire in act IV will permit Molière to expand the profound source of Dom Juan's comic nature to a similar misreading of the relationship of God to man, in another mistaken application of the dialectic of obligation.

Situations of life-and-death that should transcend the dialectic of obligation occur in every episode of the third act, which structurally telescopes and repeats three times the overall dramatic pattern of act II. The first two acts contain single situations, Dom Juan's flight from Elvire and his attempted seduction of the peasant girls. Act III, by contrast, contains no extended episode. Four incidents induce a comic rhythm, where Dom Juan's enjoyment and frustration, his euphoric inflation and deflation alternate. The structure is basic to Molière's plays and is most apparent in *L'École des femmes*. It contributes to the comic nature of the action, but as a factor of dramaturgy, not of the philosophic "comic vision" of the play. Dom Juan finds a scornful pleasure in discussing beliefs with Sganarelle; then the hermit's lesson in charity embarrasses him. He enjoys the ironies of his incognito after rescuing Dom Carlos, but loses the advantage when his own life is spared in turn. Finally, the Statue of the Commander accepts his mockingly extended invitation: the rest of the play works out the full deflation, and destruction, of Dom Juan as part of the comic rhythm pattern. In all these incidents death is an element. Dom Juan and Sganarelle joke about how doctors kill; they meet a man starving to death and learn of dangerous bandits in the wood. Carlos is nearly killed. Alonse demands Dom Juan's life on the spot. The act ends at the tomb of a man killed, not by doctors but by Dom Juan. The recurrent structural detail, and the consequent expectation that Dom Juan's euphoria and mockery at the tomb will eventually be followed by his deflation lend to the audience feelings of excitement—how will Molière arrange the deferred comeuppance?—and of assurance that the character it condemns will not triumph. If ancient tragedy uses dark oracles to prefigure the inevitable ending, Molière follows a classical esthetic and uses patterns of structure.

When act III begins, Dom Juan and Sganarelle are disguised, and Molière draws attention to Sganarelle's doctor costume by recalling Dom Juan's intention of exchanging clothing with his valet. The doctor suit permits an apparently casual reintroduction of the theme of life-and-death. Doctors, master and man agree, are not committed to saving life: their privileges alone count, and they may kill with impunity, demanding, and getting, boundless admiration and gratitude. Sganarelle believes in medicine because of the measureless consideration it confers on a doctor, even an impostor dressed as one. He believes in heaven, hell, the devil and the bogeyman for similar reasons: they are beyond him, and he stands in awe of them. Molière juxtaposes the beliefs on medicine and religion to suggest analogous qualities in the reasoning beneath the apparent foolishness of Sganarelle's argument. As the peasants bow to a man dressed in the mystery-bearing costume of a doctor, treating him with boundless respect no matter what in fact he is or does, so Sganarelle thinks of heaven as wondrously mysterious. Whether the doctor saves or kills the patient, he performs incomprehensible acts. Analogously, man and the world are full of mystery; they must have been created by a being whose nature and action, like the doctor's, are incomprehensible, before whose measureless power and essence Sganarelle bows in wonderment. Sganarelle trips himself up in farcical conclusion; the pratfall is an absurd counterpart of the moral attitude implied by his reasoning.

The argument from necessity and mystery is not original to Sganarelle. It may be taken as typical of a school of believers, including Pascal, who find in infinite *grandeur* and infinitesimal *petitesse* reasons, though irrational, for belief in God. But Sganarelle is no spokesman for any formal or popular theological position; his function is dramaturgic, to furnish a contrast for Dom Juan's rationalist credo: "Je crois, Sganarelle, que deux et deux sont quatre, et que quatre et quatre sont huit." Belief is simplified to the measurable and predictable. Dom Juan refuses to acknowledge what Sganarelle claims to be immeasurable, for which arithmetic—logical rationality—cannot account. (He would like to be limitless himself, hence the wish for new worlds to conquer, like Alexander; but Elvire's intrusion deflates the wish.) Sganarelle seems to state the position of the "esprit de finesse," lacking, however, the clarity of intuition and expression typical of this mode of perception, while Dom Juan states a case for the "esprit de géométrie," with the significant difference that he refuses to accept the promptings of intuition as a base on which to reason. Molière is not aping or parodying Pascal: the *Pensées* were not published until 1670. But could he have had prior knowledge of them? Molière seems to present a brief for what Henri Gouhier calls "un humanisme chrétien en train de tourner au christianisme humanisé."[2] At the least, Molière was familiar with the ideological context of *libertinage* whose terms Pascal knew and used. Molière's strategy parallels Pascal's, presenting two postures of the human mind, both of which separately are inadequate. Dom Juan's belief in "arithmetic" corresponds to his refusal to acknowledge and deal with obligations that are not strictly measurable and payable (even though he will not honor them either). He resists the notion of the infinite, since in that perspective nothing differentiates him from Sganarelle, or from Pierrot: "Dans la vue de ces infinis, tous les finis sont égaux" (Pensée 72). The dialectic of obligation itself withers in the face of the infinite. But while Dom Juan may shrug off Sganarelle's questions about heaven, the devil, and the bogeyman, just as he ignores relationships that conform to no manageable dialectic of obligation unless he holds the immeasurable advantage, his refusal to acknowledge belief does not mean that heaven, at least, does not exist, nor that the fact ever escapes him. To cite Pascal once more, "Tout ce qui est incompréhensible ne laisse pas d'être" (Pensée 430), and one could probably find a similar position in the Lucretian sources of seventeenth-century Epicurean *libertinage*.

The contrast between two and two are four, and the marvelous, inexplicable, and immeasurable, along with Dom Juan's pleasure over Sganarelle's clumsiness when he sees his servant trip, provide the context for the encounter with the Poor Man. As Dom Juan observes, Sganarelle's reasoning about the mystery defying reason has made them lose their way. They must seek help from the poor hermit who happens to be there when they need him. If his directions

2. Henri Gouhier, "L'Inhumain Dom Juan," *La Table ronde* 119:67–73.

are viewed in the perspective of the dialectic of obligation, the debt is measurable: eventually, Dom Juan could find a way out of the wood; and an equivalent gesture could easily be found in a piece of money or food. (If the forest is a symbolic place, signifying the perilous darkness of Dom Juan's soul, the debt is boundless. But seeing the scene as allegorical creates dramatic inconsistencies—until one realizes that the whole play is an allegory of divine charity. That will become clearer later in the discussion.) There is a greater peril to Dom Juan, and the warning about thieves in the wood, added by the hermit, engenders a much greater sense of debt in the dialectic of obligation, for it concerns life-and-death: "Mais je vous donne avis que vous devez vous tenir sur vos gardes, et que depuis quelque temps il y a des voleurs ici autour." Dom Juan's studiedly polite reply is meant to counter his debt in words: "Je te suis bien obligé, mon ami, et je rends grâce de tout mon coeur." The hermit says "je vous donne"; Dom Juan answers with "rendre," paying for precious advice with a polite formula, like Harpagon. While a coin would be more appropriate compensation to an obvious pauper, Dom Juan remains unmoved by the man's appearance. He combines polite words with the familiar "tu"—Sganarelle had used "vous"— to mark a *bonhomie* the Poor Man cannot use. The hermit then asks for charity. He needs alms to survive, like any hermit under vows of poverty: he is not without reason called "Francisque" in the cast of characters, even though the name is not spoken. (Did his costume suggest a mendicant's habit?) Dom Juan interprets the plea as a demand within the dialectic of obligation: "Ah! ah! je vois que ton avis est intéressé."

Dom Juan attacks the hermit's principles to distract from his own embarrassment, caused by the beggar's lesson in charity: "grâce" is not rendered through words, but in a saving deed or gesture that shows the effect of being touched by grace. All the fatuity and absurdity of Dom Juan's polite formula, "je te rends grâce de tout mon coeur," is revealed when he fails to respond to the hermit's obvious need. His heart is not touched. Neither he nor Sganarelle, each unmoved by tales of the doctors' victims, is capable of pity or conversion. Sganarelle even takes his master's part with the hermit, having learned his lesson after sympathizing with the peasants in act II. To cover his lack of charity, Don Juan resorts to schemes of finite obligations, like a bookkeeper tallying debts and credits in the mode of two and two are four, a concept unknown to the hermit faced with the peril of imminent starvation. Despite that concern, though, he is moved to caution two strangers about thieves in the wood; such warning, perhaps saving their life, cannot be compensated for within the bounded dialectic of obligation. Thinking in his usual manner, Dom Juan must feel himself once more in a situation of measureless debt, the kind he cannot acknowledge without recognizing his own smallness.

But Dom Juan is mistaken, for the hermit's request for alms cuts through the dialectic of obligation. He is in dire need: "Hélas, Monsieur, je suis dans la plus grande nécessité du monde"; "je vous assure, Monsieur, que le plus souvent je n'ai pas un morceau de pain à me mettre sous les dents." No one starving in a forest beats around the bush serving a potential benefactor with warnings in order to create a debt repayable with money or food. He straightforwardly asks for charity, just as the grasshopper loses all shyness when she realizes she may starve to death. (The *cigale* shows she understands the uncharitable nature of the ant when she offers to repay principal and interest, within the dialectic of obligation!)

The hermit does not argue with Dom Juan, but, insisting on his poverty and vocation, promises to respond gratefully to alms: "Je suis un pauvre homme, Monsieur, retiré tout seul dans ce bois depuis dix ans, et ne manquerai pas de prier le Ciel qu'il vous donne toute sorte de biens." Since Dom Juan is incapable of charitable giving, and because the hermit needs help, he answers Dom Juan's rebuff in terms similar to those of the dialectic of obligation, but on the infinite level that Dom Juan cannot bear. His life saved by Dom Juan's alms, he will pray for Dom Juan's salvation in a measureless sense. For a coin, the hermit will return something of infinite value well beyond two and two are four, adding to the debt already existing. Dom Juan is close to realizing an enormous return on his investment, winning the sweepstakes as it were; but the grand seigneur cannot be bettered by a hermit, even if he comes out the winner.

Both the hermit and Dom Juan are in mortal peril, though in different senses. The dark wood in traditional literature suggests the peril of the soul, from which only a figure of love as *caritas* can bring rescue, like Beatrice when she sends Vergil to Dante. This is another source of wonder, like the mysteries Sganarelle alluded to. That traditional meaning may color the hermit scene. Even without this coloring, however, the subject of the encounter remains charity in extreme situations of life-and-death. Dom Juan immediately, and deliberately, confuses the issue, making the hermit's warning seem intended to oblige him to pay a coin in return; he reads the warning as a civil gesture, without sensing the abyss between offering snuff and giving charity. Advice and coin are parts of a system of ethical values involved in the saving of life: and *the saving of life is the most exalted manner of imitating God.* This is no dialectic of obligation, but Charity with a capital C. The hermit, nearly a dead man whom Dom Juan can revive, invites Dom Juan to act according to an analogon with God that Dom Juan cannot understand because he misinterprets God's relationship to man as following the dialectic of obligation. God, however, does not push snuff. Dom Juan refuses to be moved to a charitable act by the Poor Man's extreme need. He is frustrated in his own terms, and, because he refuses to acknowledge charity, he is not converted to a system of values that would free him from the stultifying dialectic of obligation that deprives him of his fullest humanity. He prefers to spare himself embarrassment by compromising the hermit's ethical values.

The Poor Man's refusal to swear again frustrates Dom Juan. By raising the subject of self-interest, Dom Juan shows his sense of debt for the hermit's advice, and he finally agrees to pay off that imagined debt, cheaply enough, with a single gold piece. Dom Juan must hand over the coin because otherwise, in his own terms, he will remain immeasurably obligated to the hermit. He wants neither to owe nor to satisfy the debt, and getting the man to swear converts the coin into a reward for the blasphemy, in a kind of unholy bargain.

Dom Juan will no longer owe, nor will he have paid the debt, and he will have destroyed the hermit's ethical values. When his brow-beating fails, he tosses the Poor Man the gold piece "pour l'amour de l'humanité," upsetting the formula "pour l'amour de Dieu" to distract from his failure. The witty saying, however, cuts sharply along double edges, for the phrase contradicts the situation where it occurs. Repayment of the debt is a totally interested act; it is not charity. Giving for love of mankind, though, without expectation of reward and desire to rid himself of his sense of debt, would be charity. Giving disinterestedly "pour l'amour de l'humanité" con-stitutes an imitation of God, who gives and restores life, in creation and salvation, without expecting his creature ever can match such gifts in return. That is the recurrent theme of Augustine's *Confessions*, and it shapes Augustinian Catholicism as practiced by a Pascal who wonders whether God asks anything of man "sinon qu'il l'aime et le connaisse" (Pensée 430). God is the greatest benefactor possible, a philanthropist in the etymological sense, outside any dialectic of obligation.

Dom Juan's witty phrase turns ironically against him as a reminder of genuine free giving; it makes us draw distinctions between, on the one hand, Dom Juan's charity-devoid attempt to conceal em-barrassment before the hermit's lesson in charity and, on the other hand, the God of charity, outside the dialectic of obligation, who gives "pour l'amour de l'humanité." The audience does not laugh at the intended stroke of wit, which instead pierces Dom Juan's desired concealment of defeat. He unwittingly parodies God's loving relationship to man, and does not understand how close he has come to escaping the dialectic of obligation with a free, disinterested act of charity. What should be a profound, religious, humanizing ex-perience, the imitation of divine love, becomes a grandiose mocking gesture meant to save face.

This episode concerning charity in the extreme situation of life-and-death expands the vision of the play to include fundamental questions of God and man. Dom Juan's willful misinterpretation of the hermit's motive at the beginning of the scene makes him miss a rare chance to understand and imitate seriously God's relationship to man, to grasp the wonderful mystery Sganarelle had vainly reasoned about. That is genuinely sad, but Dom Juan remains comic. A tragic protagonist would face his shame and humiliation on understanding the significance of his action; he would convert to the ethical values implicit in the act whose form he had imitated, albeit unwittingly; and he then would face the consequences of conversion, whatever they might be, whatever the values might demand. That is the mechanism of Cornelian conversion and of Rotrou's *Saint Genest*, where the metaphor of performance as imitation is extended to the utmost limit: Genest learns to grasp the ethical content implicit in the play of conversion and martyrdom that he acts out. But Dom Juan remains dominated by the need to maintain the appearances of a dignity he lacks, not only when measured against God's infinite worth, but also when placed on the scale of the Poor Man, whose scruples are firm. He resists conversion, which could confer dignity, even though almsgiving closely imitates the divine act that should convert him, and us. Insistence on the dialectic of obligation, refusal to entertain the notion of free giving, determination to destroy the hermit's ethic, based on hope in God's loving charity: these deprive Dom Juan of an opportunity to correct a false perspective that condemns him to live without the full humanity he is capable of as one of God's creatures. But he is still not deprived of God's love or grace, since, although he misses the chance afforded by the crucial encounter with the Poor Man, it is not the last time Dom Juan is offered an opportunity to be moved and to act charitably in knowing or unwitting imitation of God.

An opportunity to save life, but not in imitation of God, arises right after Dom Juan tosses the Poor Man a coin. He may rush to rescue Dom Carlos because "la partie est inégale, et je ne dois pas souffrir cette lâcheté"; but he bore easily enough with unequal odds as he and Sganarelle ganged up on the hermit. Dom Juan creates an immeasurable debt of life that he does not expect Carlos to repay. Still disguised as a country gentleman, Dom Juan savors a private comedy of ironies, with the man seeking to kill him owing him life.

Molière develops the scene (III, iii) to expand on Dom Juan's pleasure in toying with the idea of infinite obligation to himself. He cuts short Carlos' speech of thanks—"Souffrez, Monsieur, que je vous rende grâce d'une action si généreuse, et que . . ."—affecting modesty, and avoiding the possibility that an expression of gratitude, a polite verbal gesture, will reduce the debt as he tried to do in response to the hermit's warning. (Pierrot's impolite verbal gesture, it may be recalled, had nullified Dom Juan's debt to him in Dom Juan's eyes.) Carlos keeps mentioning the obligation after Dom Juan admits friendship with the man Carlos pursues:

> c'est bien la moindre chose que je vous doive, après m'avoir sauvé la vie . . .

> après ce que je vous dois, ce me serait une trop sensible douleur que vous fussiez de la partie . . .

> Faut-il que je vous doive la vie, et que Dom Juan soit de vos amis?

Dom Juan's pleasure evaporates during Carlos' debate with his brother on vengeance, when Carlos satisfies the debt Dom Juan had presumed to be immeasurable and unpayable. He is no longer "redevable de la vie" to Dom Juan, for, as two and two are four, so one life spared compensates for a life saved, one infinite value equals another. From the position of superiority and arrogance implicit in his private comedy, Dom Juan is diminished as Carlos satisfies, within the dialectic of obligation, a life-and-death debt. The debate between the brothers serves a dramatic purpose more important than the analysis of aristocratic behavior and vendetta, for it reduces Dom Juan to silence and shrinks his advantage to nothing.

Dom Juan voices vexation in his response to Carlos: "Je n'ai rien exigé de vous, et vous tiendrai ce que j'ai promis." In the light of the hermit scene, there may be another unwitting parody of God in these words, with Dom Juan pretending that he had not meant to obligate Carlos by saving his life. Of course he had not demanded that Carlos be sure to "rendre le bien que j'ai reçu de vous"; he should have preferred an attack by Elvire's brothers, less threatening than the band of thieves just driven off, to losing advantage over

Carlos. He also vents rage on Sganarelle, whose scatological reply distracts from Dom Juan's frustration, allowing him, and the audience, to start building toward another brief life-and-death episode, in which pleasure is succeeded by disappointment, surprise, and fear. Molière uses jokes to make the audience lose track of Dom Juan's discomfort, duplicate his euphoria, and react more strongly when his pleasure vanishes. The comic rhythm generates a quasi identification betweeen protagonist and public. We recognize, however, that the euphoria is short-lived; and when the Statue agrees to come to dinner, we may be shocked by the supernatural element but are hardly surprised by the dramaturgy.

Dom Juan's invitation to the Statue parodies polite gesture. To the objection that visiting a man he killed is not "civile," Dom Juan argues, "Au contraire, c'est une visite dont je lui veux faire civilité, et qu'il doit recevoir de bonne grâce, s'il est galant homme." He goes "au-devant du souhait," as it were, like Sganarelle with the snuffbox, in a parody of civil behavior to obligate the Statue to himself, silly as that seems. Fresh from frustration with Dom Carlos, Dom Juan needs to be someone's creditor, even a statue's, as a concomitant of his sense of perpetual debt to God; and he desperately needs to amuse himself to forget the frustrations of his encounters with the Poor Man and Carlos. So he mocks the vanity of the Commander dressed as a Roman emperor in a grandiose tomb.

The measure of his frustration and despair is indicated by his reduction to parodying civil gestures with a statue, which, he is certain, cannot repay the simple, measurable obligation in an invitation to dinner. The scale of his gesture is radically reduced from the infinite scale of saving life on which the rest of act III occurs. But even the foolproof joke backfires and grows to that scale; the parody of ordinary civil gestures which conceal a latent will to dominate turns on Dom Juan and destroys him. The Statue will not only come to dinner, but will return the favor; and at the end of act v he will come for his guest as another civil gesture, just as Dom Juan parodically offers to see out his guests in act IV. Dom Juan calls the Statue to life, in another possible unwitting parody of divine action. In fact, though, the Statue is given movement as a divine miracle meant to restore Dom Juan to life—or to lead him to hell should he refuse conversion. True to the pattern of act III, Dom Juan's expectations about a debt that cannot be satisfied are frustrated; and the social debt, within the ordinary dialectic of obligation, that he had parodied to his surprise becomes one on the immeasurable scale of life-and-death. But Dom Juan misunderstands, as usual, fearing to incur an immeasurable debt, and refuses to convert. The parody of civil gesture that backfires sets in motion the mechanism of the Statue; and death, which spans the act from the doctor jokes to the substantial presence of the commander's funeral monument, will overarch the rest of the play.

From the parody of civil gesture in Sganarelle's snuff speech the action has led to Dom Juan's parodic gestures directed to the Statue. In act IV Dom Juan uses quasi-polite and parodic gestures to defuse the serious purpose of four unwelcome visitors, variants of the device of intruding *fâcheux*, who keep Dom Juan from enjoying distractions like those in acts II and III. He cannot dine in peace, even after dismissing the intruders with marks of courtesy, or impertinence, in the guise of civil gestures. In extending hospitable invitations to be seated—which recall his frustration in being kept from sitting at the table—or to stay for the night, or to be seen out by a punctilious host, his purpose concerns his advantage, not the comfort or pleasure of the guest. Superficial gestures are intended to manipulate obligations and avoid paying serious ethical debts.

In one recurrent gesture, Dom Juan offers to see out his guests. The "flambeau pour conduire Monsieur Dimanche," ordered by Dom Juan, occurs metaphorically in Dom Louis's speech: ancestral glory is "un flambeau qui éclaire aux yeux d'un chacun la honte de vos actions." Elvire leaves before Dom Juan can see her out: "ne faites aucune instance pour me conduire et songez seulement à profiter de mon avis," she says, rejecting polite gestures that defuse serious concerns. The Statue also rejects any accompaniment: "on n'a pas besoin de lumière, quand on est conduit par le ciel." (We shall see how the Statue returns the gesture at the end of act v, when the image of the torch is extended, in a familiar baroque poetic process, to match Dom Juan's torch in the flames of hell to which the Statue leads him.) After the first, farcical episode where Dom Juan dazzles Monsieur Dimanche, his civil, but cheap, gestures turn against Dom Juan, who cannot deflect the visitors' intention of counseling him.

The style for dealing with intruders is announced before Monsieur Dimanche enters. "Il est bon de les payer de quelque chose, et j'ai le secret de les renvoyer satisfaits sans leur donner un double." Faced, as it were, with a financial "lord" who wants an obligation honored—a meaning implicit in the derivation of "Dimanche" from *dominus*—Dom Juan substitutes imagined ethical values by insisting on the chair and by inquiring about his creditor's health and family. He raises in Dimanche a sense of boundless obligation to keep him from mentioning the finite material obligation. Dom Juan toys with the acknowledgment of his debt—puns run rampant on a vocabulary of interest, obligation, and profit—which, after all, belongs to the measurable mode of two and two are four, while he produces a sense of ethical worth in Dimanche, infinitely superior in nature to worth based on wealth. The merchant's reply, "Nous vous sommes infiniment obligés," is entirely accurate. "Tant de civilités et tant de compliments" render him ineffective as a moneylender collecting debts: paralyzed, he cannot follow his best interest, for fear that materialist concerns might diminish Dom Juan's esteem.

The instant replay between Monsieur Dimanche and Sganarelle shows in brutal terms what the master thinks of the creditor. Sganarelle throws him out; and his offer, "Je vais vous éclairer," refers less to torchlight than to enlightenment concerning Dom Juan's, and Sganarelle's, intention. The episode with Dimanche, interpolated by Molière into the plot of his sources, provides an easy victory for Dom Juan and furnishes a context for Dom Louis's visit, and for Dom Juan's impertinent put-down in the form of a "sit-down." In other circumstances, the remark, "Monsieur, si vous étiez assis, vous en seriez mieux pour parler," would denote respect for a father; here, it marks contempt, and is meant to distract from Dom Juan's vexation. His shifts from ethical concerns to a superficial polite gesture, however, cannot counter ethical debts to a father as progenitor, protector, counselor. Dom Juan's civil–contemptuous gestures with his father and with Elvire lend him no advantage: as in the hermit scene, *the audience does not laugh*, and even Sganarelle, shocked, disapproves. The dramaturgic strategy allows Dom Juan no immediate diversion. Embarrassing visits rapidly follow and are not defused by his interruptions. Dom Louis's long speech conditions us for Elvire's subsequent plea for conversion; both speeches, and the Statue's visit, stand out from their immediate contexts, which involve Sganarelle in brief episodes of farce that do not allow Dom Juan sufficient distraction.

The father's entrance stops the action. He analyzes Dom Juan's behavior and expounds a scheme of relationships governing men in the kingdom. He, and later Elvire, restate and develop themes of self-interest, obligation, and charity. But Dom Louis is not saintly; he is dominated by self-interest. Each stage of his quasi-Cornelian tirade dwells on his shame. His values exclude genuine conversion: Dom Juan is told to reform to restore the family's good name as a matter of conformity, not as a result of a change of heart. (This point of view is hardly Cornelian.) Self-interest frames his words: he had begged heaven for a son, he will implore heaven to destroy that son to purge his shame. His appeal to ancestral honor is not advice freely given for love of Dom Juan—the phrase "tendresse paternelle" seems out of place in the speech—but is intended to restore his own rank and honor at court. He is alarmed that he caused heaven to act not through grace in giving him a son but to rid itself of a pest, that he has invited punishment through his son's behavior, and that his self-interest has been justly rewarded: "ce fils, que j'obtiens en fatiguant le Ciel de voeux, est le chagrin et le supplice de cette vie même dont je croyais qu'il devait être la joie et la consolation." The king also has lost patience:

> De quel oeil, à votre avis, pensez-vous que je puisse voir cet amas d'actions indignes, dont on a peine, aux yeux du monde, d'adoucir le mauvais visage, cette suite continuelle de méchantes affaires, qui nous

réduisent, à toutes heures, à lasser les bontés du Souverain, et qui ont épuisé auprès de lui le mérite de mes services et le crédit de mes amis?

Within a surviving feudalism and according to the dialectic of obligation, royal protection and aristocratic privileges represent payment for services. A second source of privilege, however, beyond the king's debt for service, lies in "bontés," royal favors. Once Dom Louis's measurable stock of credits is exhausted, he is reduced to begging for favors—as he had begged heaven for a son—and thus risking the king's displeasure. This second relationship of noble to king, outside the dialectic of obligation, cuts to the quick of the play. While the king satisfies debts for services rendered, he may grant favors because he loves the subject; but he may be wearied by importunate pleas, and the result may resemble heaven's "favor," extended not out of grace and love, but to teach a moral lesson in the monster that is Dom Juan. Molière used analogical reasoning in Sganarelle's argument in act III and does again here.

Once the king has honored his debts, the noble, subscribing to the dialectic of obligation, stands naked of value before him. Only the sovereign's grace can restore his dignity. His service had distinguished him from common people, but now he senses the enormous gap separating him from the king. The notion here is that there is no intrinsic worth, that only continued service can establish and maintain merit; this conception is worthy of Corneille, whose protagonists successfully enhance their nature through action. The dialectic of obligation had spared the noble the acknowledgment of the essential difference between himself and the sovereign. That explains Dom Juan's need to maintain and manipulate the dialectic of obligation; like us all, he cannot bear to contemplate himself as inferior in nature or reduced in stature.

These issues are related to those raised in the critical encounter with the Poor Man. The qualitative difference between sovereign and noble, as between God and creature, cannot be measured; the mode of being of one is not statable in terms of the other. Dom Juan refuses to contend with a measureless gap beyond which infinite power and being exist. He refuses to risk the moral paralysis of feeling reduced to nothing against the limitless value of king and God, and he concludes that only two and two are four makes sense in order to keep the vast difference in nature between himself and God–king from overwhelming him. He refuses, where he is concerned, to concede the gap in the great chain of being between the creator and the created which does not permit the continuity along the chain throughout creation to extend from creation upward to God. Dom Juan unwittingly imitated God's charity with the Poor Man; now it can be observed that, where others are concerned, he manipulates the dialectic of obligation as a deliberate parodic imitation of king and God to prove a gap in nature between himself and his victims. But that gap, unlike the one in the great chain of being between creator and creation, does not exist: Molière's Dom Juan never succeeds in establishing superiority. The specious ethical value he pretends to confer makes only a Charlotte or a Dimanche sense a gulf conjured up between them and the great lord; only they are rendered ineffectual before the parodically grace-ful lending of value that bridges such a gap, and emphasizes it. Dom Juan predicts Monsieur Dimanche's response on the model of his own—if he would allow himself to acknowledge his worthlessness in the perspective of king and God. But critical differences distinguish Dom Juan's conception of divine and royal relationships to creature and subject from seventeenth-century humanistic views, including Pascal's, according to which neither God nor king commands total abnegation of value from the creature or subject. And while Dom Juan acts through self-interest to paralyze his victims, God and king exercise grace to free their chosen. Dom Juan's signs of value remain gestural, empty, parodic; God's and the king's confer genuine worth derived from, but not diminishing, their own transcendent absolute value.

Father and son, Dom Louis and Dom Juan, mistakenly explain grace and favor with parameters of human behavior that promote moral paralysis in a super-dialectic of obligation. Grace and favor, however, are freely given: *per-donare, par-don, for-give,* through gift.

They are extended for mysterious love of the creature—"pour l'amour de l'humanité"—to bridge the gap, to convert man so he may acknowledge and emulate in imitation, not parody, superior modes of being and begin to merit his redemption through actions imitative of the charity that touched the heart in conversion. These terms, reminiscent of Pascal and Corneille's strategy, are incompatible with the dialectic of obligation. They obviate the desire to indemnify others, by the gestural equivalents of offering snuff in daily life, and to forget the essential differences from God or king. In this light, the prayer "Forgive us our debts as we forgive our debtors" is pointless, for the context of grace and favor eliminates awareness of debt to God; we forgive our debts when, converted, we realize that pardon is the proper imitation of God, a form of charity. When we stop imagining God's relationship to us as a dialectic of obligation we can imitate God and grow closer to our prelapsarian nature; we begin to bridge the unclosable gap in the chain of being between God and man.

Molière's thought implicit in Dom Louis's speech draws upon Augustinian assumptions: God loves man in spite of sinfulness and fallen nature; to be restored to his nature before the Fall, man must recognize and respond to God's love; happiness consists of the imitation of God's charity subsequent to the recognition of God's love. This vision, of which Dom Louis remains unaware because of his self-interest, is extended and developed by Elvire. She comes to convert Dom Juan for love of him, in the sense of love as charity. The arrangement of her speech marks that concern. Its first section ends on the note of her lack of self-interest in visiting him: "[le Ciel] n'a laissé dans mon coeur pour vous qu'une flamme épurée de tout le commerce des sens, une tendresse toute sainte, un amour détaché de tout, qui n'agit que pour soi, et ne se met en peine que de votre intérêt." Dom Juan's mocking aside to Sganarelle, "Tu pleures, je pense," meant to distract from his embarrassment, only draws attention to the words "votre intérêt." After the interruption Elvire again stresses detachment, and begs for Dom Juan's conversion, as if her ultimate happiness were at stake.

De grâce, Dom Juan, accordez-moi, pour dernière faveur, cette douce consolation; ne me refusez point votre salut, que je vous demande avec larmes; et si vous n'êtes point touché de votre intérêt, soyez-le au moins de mes prières, et m'épargnez le cruel déplaisir de vous voir condamné à des supplices éternels.

Sganarelle's aside, "pauvre femme," highlights a notion related to the king's favor and God's grace in the phrase "accordez-moi, pour dernière faveur." Dom Juan's salvation is posed as a favor extended to Elvire outside the dialectic of obligation. Her interest lies mysteriously in *his* salvation; by converting he would act analogously to king and God, who act without self-interest for the good of the subject and creature. Like the hermit, Elvire gives him an opportunity to imitate non-parodically God and king, and to escape the dialectic of obligation. She also places her beatitude in his hands, identifying her self-interest with his salvation. Elvire is in the literary tradition of female Christian mediators, deriving from Augustine's mother, Saint Monica, and self-interest cannot properly be attributed to her. She brings into sharp focus, through her example and her pleading, the meaning of concepts found in Dom Louis's speech; and she offers a non-miraculous means of persuading Dom Juan to convert. The miracle of the Statue is an intervention of power, and a show of the lengths to which God will go to make the wayward creature convert. Elvire's attempt to convert Dom Juan is mysterious, but not miraculous. Her words suggest that the ethical life and happiness, promised by Sganarelle through snuff, are found by imitating God: "Pour l'amour de vous, ou pour l'amour de moi," Elvire pleads, echoing "pour l'amour de l'humanité" and the lesson of charity. She risks Dom Juan's scorn, but, like the Poor Man, does not allow humiliation to dissuade her from charitable actions.

Dom Juan's contempt, particularly for departures from expected social behavior in other people, means nothing to her in the light of her conversion to ethical values. That is why she advises Dom Juan, on entering, not to comment on her unusual clothing—she is veiled—as he had in act I. She must have overheard his remark then as she entered: "est-elle folle, de n'avoir pas changé d'habit, et de venir en ce lieu-ci avec son équipage de campagne?" (The comment introduces the theme of clothing, dear to the Renaissance, which has not been followed in this discussion.) As she wards off attention to meaningless conventions of dress, so she declines and avoids Dom Juan's gestures of hospitality, refusing to stay for the night—an extension of offers to sit—or to be seen out. With social debts on a petty scale Dom Juan would counter or defuse the ethical obligation he mistakenly sees in Elvire's wish to convert him. It is true that she conjures up the dialectic of obligation by referring to a "récompense" in the last section of her speech; but a dialectic whose terms, Dom Juan's salvation and Elvire's happiness, are infinite, is no dialectic but a stasis of equal, eternal terms. Dom Juan cannot reduce, through parodic civil gestures, the enormity of what Elvire freely offers him, with no interest in being his creditor. In this, she resembles the God who purified her heart.

Nor can Dom Juan succeed in mocking the Statue, who visits in response to his invitation. The Statue enters in a context of farce: Dom Juan has asked Sganarelle to sit at dinner with him—a gesture showing the real significance, as mocking shows of courtesy, of other invitations to sit since he has the dishes removed before Sganarelle can touch them. Sganarelle serves again as a scapegoat for the embarrassment brought by Dom Louis and Elvire. Dom Juan extends courtesies to the Statue by asking Sganarelle to join the feast, to sing, and to toast the Commander's health, another contemptuous gesture, since the Commander is dead and Dom Juan killed him! The perfect host's every courteous gesture within the dialectic of obligation is designed to cover his amazement and to increase his guest's debt, while his commands to Sganarelle reveal the parodic nature of the gestures, meant to frighten the valet and to offend the Statue. But the Statue remains faithful to the dialectic of obligation initiated in the graveyard: he acquits himself of liability, no matter how contemptuous the original indebting gesture, by inviting Dom Juan in turn to dine. He delivers no moralizing speech, as the audience expects according to the pattern set by Dom Louis and Elvire (that speech is deferred until the end when the Statue, as host, may choose the subject of conversation, as it were); but the earlier visitors came for Dom Juan's reform, while the Statue visits because he is obliged to, in response to an invitation accepted.

The forces at play here are greater than in previous scenes, no less than divinity and death, infinite though concretized in the Statue. They nevertheless obey the comparatively petty laws of the dialectic of obligation; and it is according to those laws, the laws of two and two are four on a level of measurable and commensurable gestures, that Dom Juan is to be destroyed: in his own terms. Whereas he should recognize the presence of infinite forces in the miraculous Statue, he refuses, and the Statue obligingly responds in the only terms Dom Juan will acknowledge. Instruments Dom Juan uses to gain advantage, parodically, over the Statue of the Commander he had killed become instruments of his own destruction. The torch, passed by Dom Juan to Sganarelle as the fourth act ends to see the Statue out, gains its full significance at the play's end when the Statue returns the gesture, within the dialectic of obligation, but on an infinite scale, as only God can: the torch is repaid boundlessly and endlessly in the fires of hell. Dom Juan is finally made to acknowledge the presence of the infinite and everlasting, when the grace and favor of heaven are shown to be exhausted. The life-and-death situation ends in death, despite the extreme charity of the Statue.

The Statue visits, it is true, because he accepted Dom Juan's invitation. But within a pattern of decreasing self-interest on the part of the fourth-act visitors, the Statue has the least self-interest: in effect, as an instrument for Dom Juan's salvation, he acts despite his own interest within the aristocratic code and the dialectic of obligation. Charity succeeds vendetta; and only when Dom Juan refuses charity is he struck down, but not even then for the Commander's vengeance. The operation of grace through the Statue portrays the effects of conversion, the loss of the Commander's self-interest, and, only finally, the effects of a refusal to convert.

Dom Juan's hypocrisy and parody of conversion provide material for act V and trigger his destruction. As a hypocrite, he intends to put off those who press for his repentance while indulging his desires and placing enemies in his power. The strategy seems to work when the act begins, for Dom Louis believes his son and praises "la bonté du Ciel" for effecting conversion. He leaves to "rendre grâce au Ciel," still thinking of heaven's free gifts in the improper terms of the dialectic of obligation. Dom Juan's hypocritical posture as heaven's defender seems successful.

In the second scene his delight on fooling his father breaks out, and he eagerly describes for Sganarelle a gamut of gestures designed to satisfy his desires à la Tartuffe while he pretends to serve others as a spiritual and ethical guide. As in his explanation of inconstancy in love in I, iii, the Alexander speech, in this long discourse he is anxious to expound his thought to Sganarelle, to justify his behavior, and to enjoy the valet's shock. Both speeches recall Sganarelle's praise of snuff. Passing around a parody of religion, Dom Juan uses heaven as Sganarelle offered snuff in a parody of civil gesture. Sganarelle provoked laughter with his claims and Gusman was unimpressed; Dom Juan seemingly offers nothing less than salvation, and nobody laughs. Dom Juan's parodic gesture would place in his debt people ready for grace and real conversion, just as Sganarelle meant to obligate the real owner of the snuffbox. But while a receiver of snuff can easily repay his benefactor in kind, no service matches the benefits of religion: eternal life and beatitude.

Dom Juan expects his gestures performed in the name of "le Ciel"—his response to Carlos' every objection in scene iii—to shield him and afford him ethical advantage. The structure of act V, a counterstructure to act IV, allows him increasing euphoria until the Spectre and the Statue appear. He refuses conversion, but for once honors his word, to join the Statue for dinner. The dialectic of obligation begun in the graveyard is thus satisfied, and the Statue, acting truly in heaven's name, leads Dom Juan to a death provoked by his refusal of grace and his abuse of heaven's name. As the sovereign must act to protect the state and his subjects from Tartuffe's ultimate crime, his false serving of the prince for his own self-interest, so heaven must renounce its grace and destroy Dom Juan for the sake of those creatures who are open to grace and salvation, lest Dom Juan's hypocrisy in the name of heaven threaten their spiritual welfare. Dom Juan receives the wages of sin because of God's love for man, "pour l'amour de l'humanité"; death, which has hovered over the play since act II, claims Dom Juan.

The matter of wages for years of service dominates Sganarelle's final, shocking speech. It contains no word of lament for his master, nor a moral. Molière concludes with a frustrated Sganarelle, bounding around the stage searching for signs of Dom Juan, demanding his wages of the air peopled with imaginary benefactors, like Harpagon pleading for his strongbox with the people he conjures up around him, then with the audience laughing at him. Sganarelle is also laughed at, as, obsessed, he shouts for his wages, again and again: at the beginning of the speech, "Mes gages! mes gages!"; at the end, "Mes gages! mes gages! mes gages!" La Grange, having disappeared through a trap door, could not have seen Molière's stage movements and may have wondered why he heard laughter following Dom Juan's damnation.

The gestural play no longer involves Sganarelle's polite offering of what was not his to obligate a circle of imagined snuff-takers. He gestures wildly to demand what is owed him in the dialectic of obligation that bound him to his master. Everyone is satisfied and content, made happy not by snuff, as it were, but by Dom Juan's death—and of course Sganarelle is wrong: no character is satisfied by Dom Juan's death. Sganarelle is left with nothing to show for his servitude, compromised by association with a wicked master. He had remained with Dom Juan in the expectation of payment: not for ethical values, but for material values contracted for and deliverable as part of a dialectic of obligation between master and servant. He is not like Sancho Panza, who remains faithful to Don Quixote long after it becomes apparent that any reward his master might bestow cannot compare with the ethical and spiritual ties between them.

Sganarelle is as comic as Dom Juan, perhaps more so, because the point escapes him. After witnessing miracles in a drama of divine charity, he can think only of the wages his master pledged to him. The last laugh is on Sganarelle, because the purveyor of snuff, cheated in the dialectic of obligation, should have learned from experience that his master never honored debts and because he is still concerned with material obligations when he, who had argued in act III for something wondrous responsible for man, has witnessed miracles of charity outside the dialectic of obligation. A comedy with reconciliation, or a tragedy, would end with a hymn to God's charity and power. But Sganarelle does not see beyond his wages. Like his master, he is totally bound to the dialectic of obligation— stultifying, reducing everything in the manner of two and two are four to the measure of only one element in man, and ultimately destructive of qualities deemed by the period of Molière and Pascal, of humanist freethinkers, noble and bourgeois gentlemen, believing philosophers and apologists for religion, to confer dignity and value on the incomprehensible monster, man.

·3·

ESTHETICS AND ETHICS
IN *LE MISANTHROPE*

Molière produced *Le Misanthrope* in 1666 while *Tartuffe* was still banned and after *Dom Juan* had been withdrawn. The latent mythology of those controversial plays concerns relationships between bountiful and loving powers—the Christian's God and his surrogate or temporal analogue, the king—and the individual man who is both creation of the God and subject of the king. Tartuffe and Dom Juan sow discord in society and family as they misinterpret and imitate perversely the bond that benevolently unites the sources of authority and the people they rule. The link between divinity and man is not at stake in *Le Misanthrope;* however, a model for the interplay amongst the characters occurs in the mysterious operations between the king and his courtiers. Given the apparent superficiality, if not utter worthlessness, of the petits marquis Clitandre and Acaste, and of Oronte, the play gives cause for wonder concerning their status. This ethical speculation on an individual's merits and the rewards he may expect or actually receive extends to three isomorphic lines of plot: Alceste's quarrels with the royal court, the law, and Célimène.

Alceste, the "hater of humanity," complements Dom Juan, the self-styled "lover of mankind." Dom Juan pretends to serve people to foster the illusion of a gap in worth and nature between himself and those whom he treats as though they possessed a superior value

73

which they know they lack. He misconstrues the intentions of God and king toward creation and subjects, and consequently views himself as burdened by an overwhelming debt that paralyzes him and denies him dignity. His obliging acts, based on that false conception, are meant to engender similar debts toward himself, so that he may ignore the nullity he mistakenly feels before authentic powers while enjoying the illusion of superiority over his fellow creatures and subjects. His "love" is not charity, but a technique of avoiding embarrassing debts of life-and-death. God and king love their creation and subjects; he loves no one.

The same misunderstanding of obligation and of love makes Alceste act dis-obligingly, with undisguised scorn for courtly conventions. Contrary to his fears, praise and flattery engender no infinite debts, but suggest that people may possess inherent and acquired ethical value and that such worth may be acknowledged by others. But Alceste doubts that such value exists, just as Dom Juan finds himself lacking when measured against the infinite and absolute worth of God and king. If man is a nullity, or if his heart is hollow and full of filth, to paraphrase Pascal, Alceste refuses to honor a noble lie or myth enabling man to act with dignity despite his natural or fallen condition. Alceste behaves disobligingly to expose worthlessness, but also to gain advantage by revealing his awareness of man's sorry state: compared to the nullity of everyone else, his ethical worth would appear infinite. What Dom Juan attempts by pretending love and service, Alceste attempts by scornful, humiliating behavior.

The first gesture in *Dom Juan*, the offering of snuff, engenders a series of movements that remind the audience of interrelated ethical themes of borrowed value, advantage and obligation. The first gestures in *Le Misanthrope* point to disobligation and humiliation. Alceste's behavior in act I toward Philinte, then Oronte, and in act II toward Acaste and Clitandre indicates a denial of their value. He tries to embarrass and humiliate them, to reveal their superficiality and lack of intrinsic merit. The others join in embraces from which he shrinks, preferring to dissolve civil society and to turn the salon, an epitome of civilization, into the wilderness where the vicious animal, man, belongs. He finally leaves the salon, depopulated not because of his intentions but as a result of the revelation of Célimène's ethical worthlessness; he moves from one void to another in his own wilderness and passes up an opportunity to convert, if not the entire society which he despises, the one person whom he claims to love. That refusal makes him profoundly comic and nonheroic, for he will not take the chance of remaining to attempt to cure Célimène's flawed nature, replacing her nullity with some ethical substance.

The setting itself should suggest the dark void that Alceste finds at the heart of man with a performance beginning and ending on an empty, unlit stage. The salon is dark at the opening (and in v, i) because Célimène is not receiving guests. Alceste has presumably just entered; he may even enter after the curtains part, followed soon after by Philinte, who does not immediately notice Alceste brooding in a corner (the same place where he will again take refuge in v, i–ii). The salon should not be fully lit until Oronte arrives, followed by a lackey with candelabras. At the end, as Philinte and Éliante pursue Alceste offstage, the empty salon is seen again, and a lackey may snuff out the candles before the curtains close. In this place vacuous people, observed by a few ironic but sympathetic commentators, gather to convince themselves of their power and influence at the salon and at a court where, inherent merit aside, everything depends upon royal favor and grace.

The court, of course, is never seen;[1] however, the characters belong to the court, not in some vague Kafkaesque sense, but in a

---

1. The closest one gets to a depiction of the court in Molière's theater is in *L'Impromptu de Versailles*, in which the king graciously spares *his* theatrical company the humiliation of performing an inadequately rehearsed play. That comedy pits the ungenerous behavior of virtually everyone— and particularly of Molière, who ridicules without mercy his rivals and detractors—against the benevolence of the sovereign. Even in an "impromptu" Molière observes the gap between king and subject. It might also be noticed that *Le Misanthrope* is Molière's only comedy whose characters are courtiers.

very real, tangible manner: these are all aristocrats with access to the powerful, and the play constantly provokes speculation on a system of politics or justice that permits such eminently worthless folk to enjoy proximity to royalty and privilege. It is impossible to ignore the status—at least the alleged status—of Célimène's suitors, for Oronte promptly announces his (I, ii, 290–92) and Acaste boasts of his (III, i, 802); Arsinoé proffers influence (III, v, 1075–80); the portrait scene, II, iv, is framed by references to the king's *lever* and *petit coucher* (567, 739). That such fools as these receive privilege remains a mystery, to audiences as well as to Alceste. Surely their vain behavior indicates no inherent worth commanding either royal favor or Célimène's love. But Alceste commits the same mistake if he believes that his intrinsic merit deserves extraordinary favor at court and in the salon. A king and a woman do not bestow favor so logically; nor must they justify their preferences. Privilege and love may inspire respect, wonder, fear, worship, and remain unexplained manifestations of what Pascal might call "la raison des effets," free of logic or jurisprudence and irreducible to mechanistic systems of cause and effect. Alceste must hate this phenomenon, for his merit, as he fancies it, is not rewarded as it would be under a justice based upon a predictable scheme of deserts and rewards—and of crimes and punishment. Like Dom Juan, Alceste demands that two and two add up to four, insisting that he embodies the virtue that a just regime would recognize. He raises the question of proven merit (in III, v, 1053–56), but ironically, to ask Arsinoé what he has done to deserve honors at court. The question occurs against the context of Acaste and Clitandre, about whom the audience must wonder: "What have they, or Oronte, done to deserve their favored places?"

Unlike the justice exercised by a king or lover, Alceste's lawsuit should operate according to established and predictable conventions. Where human behavior is involved, Dom Juan's insistence on finite sums should be respected. While Alceste demands that the law be rigorously applied, however, he refuses to respect conventions that operate as a kind of "raison des effets": one tries to influence judges because such behavior is expected. To gain advantage, one acknowledges their power. Judges are unlike God and king, who remain unconcerned with advantage, whose power is infinite, and who need no such acknowledgment of power, for a unit added to infinity does not increase infinity. Men do need and do respond to such tributes; they insist, albeit mistakenly, that men treat them with deference as though they were gods wholly concerned with avowals of their power. The man suing Alceste, as perverse as Tartuffe, visits judges to gain advantage; he uses the mechanism, humiliating himself, and wins the case because, like virtually everyone in the society, he behaves according to a common false interpretation of the bond between the bountiful powers and man. Alceste, however, is just as bad, for although he refuses to compromise and to flatter the powerful, he demands that his inherent worth be accorded its due as a matter of some inalienable right; and he makes those demands in court, law court, salon—and, by extension, Célimène's bedroom.

In Célimène's salon similar modes of behavior are shaped by criteria of misunderstood grace and advantage. The suitors expect her to acknowledge their inherent merit. This idea of love resembles their confusion of the king's awarding privilege to them by grace with their expectations of reward for inherent worth. Their nullity goes unperceived by them, although the audience must conclude that their attention to superficial details of dress and manner covers up something missing, some gap in nature between their illusions about themselves and their reality. They do not understand that advantage depends entirely on the king and on Célimène—call it grace or caprice. Alceste is more like the marquis and Oronte than he might care to observe. They all apply perversely in the salon the paradigm of the court. And given the implicit royal approval of the noblemen whom Alceste denounces, the condemnations gain an additional ludicrous dimension: what gives Alceste the right to denounce what the king honors? Like Pascal, Alceste perceives nullity; he refuses, however, to entertain the possibility of transforming these hearts through the mysterious operations of grace. He understands the conventions, but misses the all-embracing context that reduces to pettiness any insistence on advantage and inherent merit.

Alceste comprehends the utility of praise: flattering Oronte may engender obligations repayable as service at court. But he insists that preferment there derive from qualities he can justly boast of, such as sincerity. Alceste exercises this inherent (or learned, or feigned) virtue, however, to humiliate; unlike a gentleman, he behaves virtuously to attract attention. Alceste's insistence on his sincerity is like the petits marquis' claim to fame. Pride in some advantage or special value—"se *vanter* de l'*avantage*," as it were—is an abuse of the quality, and it might be argued that an implicit pun between se *vanter* and *avantage* governs the comic nature of *Le Misanthrope*'s characters and plot. Each character boasts of advantage as though it existed through some merit that justified flaunting. Advantage, however, is not produced by inherent worth, but at court by the chances of birth and royal favor, and in the salon by the choices of some arbiter of values (or fashions). Alceste's proud insistence on his virtuous refusal to praise and embrace also makes him forget the dynamics of the act he resists, for the praiser-embracer gains advantage by creating obligations. Such debts are easily repaid in kind, as Philinte observes early in the play (I, i, 37–40), and boasting of such an advantage would be pointless. No one takes so seriously as Alceste the convention of praising and embracing, to which, nevertheless, everyone subscribes as one of the main structures supporting society.

In its first scenes *Le Misanthrope* elicits by language and visible gestures the audience's awareness of the ethical issues and relationships that the characters misinterpret and abuse. Alceste accompanies his repeated swearing—"morbleu," "parbleu"—with some untoward gesture inappropriate to a salon. Some characters embrace—the two marquis in III, i, Célimène and Arsinoé in III, iii—in real or pretended friendship, while Alceste shuns Oronte's offers of embracing (I, ii). Alceste is the first character to mention the gesture, exaggerating its importance as he narrates the incident that has offended him: Philinte enthusiastically greeted and praised some man he barely knew. When Molière played Alceste, in describing that event twice using specific, then more general terms (I, i. 14–28, 41–64), he must have acted it out, imitating with exaggeration Philinte's embracing in the farcical manner of the Italian commedia dell'arte. Alceste's mocking movement and language are meant to humiliate Philinte (as well as to produce laughter in the audience). This attempt to embarrass Philinte fails, however, for he makes light of Alceste's conclusion: "Et si par un malheur j'en avais fait autant, / Je m'irais, de regret, pendre tout à l'instant" (27–28). Philinte laughs off the condemnation: "Je ne vois pas, pour moi, que le cas soit pendable" (29); and he introduces the principle of grace that governs divine and royal justice: "Que je me fasse un peu grâce sur votre arrêt" (31). In the second, more general version, Alceste observes that there can be no advantage if everyone, high, low, worthy, worthless, is praised and embraced. He is correct; but he misses the point that the embracer creates his own advantage in an obligation. Alceste imitates from a mistaken angle an act that connotes advantage: he mechanically assumes the viewpoint of the person embraced and praised—a position he believes only he deserves. If he had wanted distinction, however, he might have adopted the other perspective, for even conventionally the praiser is superior by the creation of debt and by a faithful representation of the archetypal relationship between the bountiful powers and their subjects. God and king confer value on whom they will; the object of such giving cannot justifiably claim credit for his salvation or elevation to dignity. In the play, only Philinte and Éliante understand this. Alceste, like the other comic figures, operates according to mistaken notions of value and praise, embracing and humiliation.

He is committed to a program of exposing the emptiness of the court, and even of his friend. But Philinte characteristically makes fun of such exaggerations as "dying of shame": "Allez, vous devriez mourir de pure honte" (14). This ridicule supplies a model for Alceste's behavior and the response to it that the play subsequently follows: his attempts to humiliate are met by outright failure, a refusal to acknowledge his intentions, or mockery. Alceste also tries to humiliate by ignoring the other person. At the beginning he snubs Philinte, who finally uses the subject of friendship to provoke Alceste into standing and arguing. Alceste deliberately looks away during Oronte's first speech to him. In the criticism of the sonnet scene he acts out another incident that lets him turn from Oronte. In act II when Acaste and Clitandre enter, he tries to embarrass Célimène, then goes alone to his corner (where he had hidden in act I and from which he will observe Oronte and Célimène in act V). In act IV he rudely snubs Philinte. In act V he remains silent during all the accusations of Célimène, as if Oronte, the two marquis, and Arsinoé were not worth his attention. Finally he dismisses Célimène in an ultimate act of humiliation. In this, too, he does not properly imitate God and king, who, one hopes, pardon unconditionally and raise the sinner despite his failings. They behave according to both Pascalian polarities: "S'il se vante, je l'abaisse; s'il s'abaisse, je le vante; et le contredis toujours jusqu'à ce qu'il comprenne qu'il est un monstre incompréhensible" (Pensée 420).

Alceste cannot deal with a hybrid nature, raising and lowering, praising and denigrating, as is apparent in his dealings with Oronte, who both vaunts his ability and pretends to submit to Alceste's superior critical acumen. Alceste of course cannot deal fairly with Oronte, being jealous of Oronte's status at court and fearing him as a rival for Célimène. On the basis of the sonnet Alceste might reasonably take less than seriously Oronte's bid for Célimène; but what irks Alceste is less Oronte's poetic gifts than his ability to impress Célimène with his rank.

Oronte's entrance diplomatically de-emphasizes his courtship, as though he wished to defuse the situation of rivals meeting on the battleground that is the salon. He sounds disappointed to miss Éliante at home, while Célimène occurs in an afterthought: "J'ai su là-bas que pour quelques emplettes / Éliante est sortie, et Célimène aussi" (I, ii, 250–51). His speeches, however, concern neither woman, but the power at court which he uses to woo Célimène. He is implying that visiting Célimène is unimportant since he need not worry about impressing her at home; he deserves Célimène by virtue of the influence at court that demonstrates his intrinsic worth. Célimène should in effect desire Oronte to choose her from amongst the women seeking him! Oronte does not suspect that he owes rank and the king's attention to royal generosity, not his own inherent deserts. His approach to Alceste reflects that misconception. He offers signs of friendship as though Alceste's value equaled his. But in return he demands recognition in Alceste's approval of the sonnet. He presents the poem as a sign of inherent worth outside the court and independent of the king. (He also presents the poem as if it were an afterthought, the same way he first refers to Célimène.) Célimène is expected to assign advantage according to her suitors' intrinsic merit, which they show in exterior forms. She is like the king and unlike him. She may act by grace but is not bound to. However, while his bounties are theoretically infinite and may be conferred on countless subjects, a woman may favor only one man (at a time). The suitors, including Alceste, dwell on this distinction; each is convinced that only he possesses that privilege by virtue of his intrinsic merit, as each misconstrues his standing with the king.

That relationship underlies the marshals' reconciliation of Alceste and Oronte, as narrated by Philinte in IV, i. Royal agents maintain order amongst aristocrats who, despite their nullity compared with the king's power after the Fronde, insist upon personal advantage to the others' detriment. The marshals force Alceste to submit to a humiliating gesture of apology: if the king favors Oronte, no subject may dispute Oronte's privilege, using his poetry as pretext. The sonnet may be an attempt to give tangible substance to the merit everyone assumes the king rewards. But, as the marshals' action indicates, it is not necessary that the privileged possess extraordinary merit, and, good, bad, or indifferent, the poetry does not count. Only the king's grace does. Oronte may mistakenly try to make the king's grace seem a reward for merits, but that does not matter either. It does, however, make him a figure of comedy.

In tacit acknowledgment of this ethos, nobody derides to their face the people Alceste scorns, such as Émilie and Dorilas, who are succinctly portrayed by Philinte (I, i, 81–86). The accidental and superficial characteristics assumed by a privileged subject are insignificant since the king countenances them. This notion corresponds to Éliante's views on lovers proposed in II, iv—a beloved's flaws are transformed into virtues—and to a philosophy according to which all values flow from an authority, royal or divine. In Christian mythological terms, values originate in a God who, through love, overlooks man's failings as a fallen creature. The Christian, particularly the Christian humanist, encourages men to do likewise, pardoning in action as he hopes he will be forgiven his sins. Alceste, on the contrary, poses as an authority opposing the king's right to honor whom he will; taking his stance one degree further to theological matters, Alceste might well challenge God's right to save the obviously undeserving.

His attitudes toward the privileged courtiers are evident as he snubs Oronte and the two marquis. He "paraît tout rêveur" during Oronte's first speech (stage direction at I, ii, 250–61) and gracelessly refuses to face his rival as though he were avoiding an encounter like the one for which he had chided Philinte. His surprise at Oronte's compliments is an ironic put-down in the context of the preceding exposition. During Oronte's continuing flattery Alceste cannot contain Oronte or himself: Oronte keeps cutting him off as he begins to object with polite repetitions of "Monsieur" (266, 269, 271, 276). These interruptions make it difficult for Alceste to ignore Oronte, or to return the compliments, were he so conventionally inclined. Oronte makes the exchange one-sided, increasing Alceste's obligation with unreciprocated praise. Alceste should prefer to minimize the debt, and he also suffers from the flattery, for Oronte couches his remarks in terms that Alceste wants to hear from people he respects, if not from the king himself. Oronte insists on Alceste's qualities that should be acknowledged at court: the man favored at the Louvre despite his apparent lack of worth flatters the man without status there who believes that he alone deserves royal honors.

Or.: L'estime où je vous tiens ne doit point vous surprendre
     Et de tout l'univers vous la pouvez prétendre.
Al.: Monsieur . . .
Or.:   L'État n'a rien qui ne soit au-dessous
     Du mérite éclatant que l'on découvre en vous.

(265–68)

This rhetoric suggests that Alceste possesses an inherent value that bursts forth brilliantly, but which, paradoxically, Oronte discerns and reveals in him. Alceste cannot bear that the praise redound upon the praiser. Oronte's language—the contradiction between "éclatant" and "on découvre"—is a hodgepodge of conventional rhetoric that flatters without attending to the real substance of things. Alceste does believe his value surpasses everyone else's; but he does not want to hear that said insincerely, rhetorically, by Oronte or Arsinoé (in III, v). Alceste's repeated "Monsieurs" do not silence Oronte; nothing will stop him short of embracing, the diametric opposite of Alceste's snubs.

Oronte stands open-armed, ready to seal pledges of friendship. Does Alceste shrink from the abhorrent gesture? If Oronte wears an oversized coat, as Célimène suggests ("l'homme à la veste," V, iv, prose between 1690 and 1691), he must seem about to engulf his rival. Does Alceste's repulsion prompt Oronte to express surprise: "Quoi! vous y résistez?" (276). Or does Alceste simply turn away? His studiedly polite answer (277–84) plays upon the conceit of friendship as a quasi-sacred relationship: "mystère," "en profaner le nom," "nous nous repentirions." Friendship is also a matter of judgment: "Avec lumière et choix cette union veut naître" (281). (Is friendship then unlike love, which reason does not govern, according to Alceste at I, i, 248?) But Alceste's elevated reasoning avoids the real issue; he does not address Oronte's qualities or flaws, and he shows how little he thinks Oronte deserves notice. He betrays his principle of blunt denunciation, although he follows his gestural program of accompanying disobliging, humiliating acts.

Oronte would obligate his new "friend" with offers of service at

83

court. He is less intent, however, on gaining Alceste's affection than in observing that his status with the king might benefit Alceste, if only Alceste would request favors or praise the sonnet. The juxtaposition of Oronte's statement about his position and the poem, which he draws from his coat, is deliberate:

> S'il faut faire à la cour pour vous quelque ouverture,
> On sait qu'auprès du roi je fais quelque figure:
> Il m'écoute, et dans tout il en use, ma foi,
> Le plus honnêtement du monde avecque moi.
> Enfin je suis à vous de toutes les manières;
> Et, comme votre esprit a de grandes lumières,
> Je viens, pour commencer entre nous ce beau noeud,
> Vous montrer un sonnet que j'ai fait depuis peu,
> Et savoir s'il est bon qu'au public je l'expose.

(289–97)

The poem reminds Alceste that Célimène favors Orgon not for mysterious reasons, as at court, but for his poetic talent that signifies intrinsic value. Neither style nor taste is at issue in the sonnet scene; the underlying subject concerns Oronte's privileges at court and, analogously, in the salon.

Oronte's request for advice about reciting the poem is *pro forma;* he will read it regardless of Alceste's evaluation, expecting praise either in response to his offers of service or to blunter allusions to power. Alceste tries to ignore the affair, to avoid the sonnet and the larger issues. Sincerity is a pretext as he declares that "j'ai le défaut / D'être un peu plus sincère en cela qu'il ne faut" (299–300). Oronte claims he wants sincerity, and asks Alceste for authoritative criticism, without, however, allowing him independent authority: Oronte states the terms he desires to hear. Alceste of course wants nothing more than to dictate all values, but not under Oronte's guidance or patronage. When Oronte insists, Alceste invents a fiction, until Oronte provokes him into a malicious critique that strikes at matters more crucial than an occasional poem. The policy of ignoring Oronte and his sonnet breaks down. Himself humiliated by his contact with Oronte and the role in which Oronte's insistence has cast him, Alceste tries to humiliate Oronte. His responses become violent in the second half of the scene, as is not surprising in a quarrel; but Molière emphasizes the violence by Alceste's earlier studied politeness.

Alceste had not objected to Oronte's introductory remarks dictating the terms in which the sonnet was to be praised:

> . . . Ce ne sont point de ces grands vers pompeux,
> Mais de petits vers doux, tendres et langoureux.

> . . . Je ne sais si le style
> Pourra vous en paraître assez net et facile,
> Et du choix des mots vous vous contenterez.
>
> (307–11)

But he had not responded with the appropriate civil gesture expected by Oronte, by praising the style in advance. Alceste remains cool. He addresses violent remarks to Philinte who praises the quatrains and tercets: "Morbleu! vil complaisant, vous louez des sottises?" (326). Alceste, enraged, directs against Philinte, that ironic agent provocateur of a friend, his sense of the humiliation to which Oronte makes him submit. Philinte's comments, breaking his silence since Oronte's entrance, and Alceste's reaction make the audience think Alceste will follow the principles of sincerity enunciated in the exposition. These exchanges reveal Alceste's violent feelings, which contrast with the manipulative politeness shown Oronte after the reading. Alceste still does not condemn the sonnet, except to Philinte. He constructs an elaborate strategy to ignore Oronte and the poem by narrating an incident undoubtedly invented on the spot: he once advised a would-be poet to preserve his reputation as a gentleman by suppressing a mania for writing. Alceste can turn from Oronte to act out his kindly role, addressing to him only the repeated phrase "Je ne dis pas cela" (352, 358, 362) as assurance that the poetaster in question is not a stand-in for Oronte.

This is not just an intelligent (albeit hypocritical) face-saving device. Alceste's notions about gentlemanly behavior reflect contemporary thought on *honnêteté*, such as the Chevalier de Méré's or

85

Pascal's; gentlemen do not pride themselves on accidentals or special talents. Alceste, however, uses the stratagem maliciously, as Célimène and Arsinoé will in act III for purposes of humiliation. In his little drama, Alceste plays a reasonable man advising an imaginary foolish interlocutor. Alceste's superiority is the point of his extended advice, along with the elusive–allusive manner of recognizing Oronte, as it were, in an indirect confrontation. Alceste continues his performance in four speeches, two of them fairly long, even after Oronte has three times seemed to get the point. Alceste enjoys the persona of reason and *honnêteté* opposed to his humiliated interlocutor. He duplicates Oronte's earlier behavior in the "Je ne dis pas cela" speeches: he claims qualities vis-à-vis the would-be poet as Oronte had boasted of his advisor's status with the king. Alceste styles himself an expert on proper behavior, an expertise which means more than the authority Oronte had flatteringly attributed to him: "comme votre esprit a de grandes lumières" (294). Alceste claims ethical, not esthetic, expertise on how to prove one's merits at court: ". . . n'allez point quitter, de quoi que l'on vous somme, / Le nom que dans la cour vous avez d'honnête homme" (369–70). Alceste manages to usurp Oronte's place as an expert on the court: he alone knows the true worth that the court should honor. But he is also aware that his theory, orthodox enough for philosophers of *honnêteté*, is not practiced: Oronte will not lose status, although his alleged friends may ridicule him covertly. These speeches are a self-indulgence of Alceste's meant to mortify Oronte slyly in Alceste's eyes. He is not forthright like the reasonable counselor he plays. Alceste acts out what he believes court behavior to be. While he does not permit Oronte to lose a sense of his importance, in his own eyes Alceste still belittles his rival.

When Oronte finally makes Alceste return to the sonnet, the act of humiliation occurs openly. "Franchement, il est bon à mettre au cabinet" (376): Alceste brutally exercises the authority Oronte had naïvely allowed him. Citing standards of "truth" and "nature" Alceste sounds straightforward. But when he turns to "le méchant goût du siècle" and twice recites (or sings) a song from the good old days of Henri IV, Oronte's talent for poetry is clearly no longer an issue or pretext. Alceste replaces the sign of Oronte's favor in the salon with something obsolete from a period when men lusted after women openly, and not with pretty conceits. The song is not an aristocrat's but one that might be on everyone's lips, and thus it could not denote anyone's privileges at court or in a salon. The criteria of "bon sens" and "passion pure" are secondary; the real thrust of the example is less in style than in a meaning which rejects the court's favors: If the king gave me Paris, I'd tell him to take it back—an idea that could be phrased more coarsely—for I prefer my love. It has been argued that Oronte's poem challenges Alceste, alluding to Oronte's hope for Célimène's favors, and that Alceste's song replies that his beloved has already rewarded him.[2] That song, however, contrasts privileges at court with reward in the salon. Oronte may expect Célimène to acknowledge his merit, which is apparent in the sonnet and to be inferred from his rank. Alceste claims that status with the king is less important than being chosen by the beloved woman. Nevertheless, the underlying issue has all along been favor at court—and only Oronte has that. The king will never give Paris to Alceste. The song describes a fantasy that distracts from the truth as Alceste pretends to ignore his own situation, just as he had tried to avoid Oronte and the sonnet. The song does not satisfy his stated criterion for poetry, fidelity to truth. Enraged by Oronte's undeserved favor at court, he uses it to reiterate that he neither needs nor wants privilege there. Alceste dissembles in the "Je ne dis pas cela" sequence of fictions, then again in the song. And if Célimène is at issue, then he is also untruthful, for she too has conferred no special status upon him.

The sonnet becomes Alceste's pretext for revenge on his rival. Oronte's undeserved favor at court, he implies, will gain him no advantage in the salon, for Célimène chooses merit. (How wrong this will turn out to be in act v!) But Alceste suffers in the dispute from the renewed realization of Oronte's rank. The polite "Mon-

2. F. W. Lindsay, "Alceste and the Sonnet," *French Review* 28:395–402.

sieurs" he had earlier proferred reecho in taunts: Oronte's "mon petit Monsieur, prenez-le un peu moins haut" and Alceste's rejoinder, "Ma foi, mon grand Monsieur, je le prends comme il faut" (433–34). These spiteful remarks clarify the situation: Alceste *is* a "petit monsieur" and Oronte *is* a "grand monsieur" at court. Civilities have broken down; bare power is invoked, humiliatingly for Alceste. Philinte's intrusion, like that of the marshals later, restores the polite jargon of advantage and service: "Je suis votre valet, Monsieur, de tout mon coeur. / —Et moi je suis, Monsieur, votre humble serviteur" (437–38). These conventional farewells pose a pseudo relationship of servant–master between equals. Intended ironically here, they imitate perversely the relationship the language denotes. Oronte had entered with offers of service; now as "votre valet" he will prove a knave to Alceste. Alceste leaves the salon to avoid Philinte's embarrassing reminders of the harmful consequences of sincerity (as if Alceste had in fact been sincere), but also to find Célimène and make her ban all courtiers from the salon. He will enjoy privileged rank there, even if it is a society emptied of its usual occupants—even if it is a kind of desert.

Alceste's view of sincerity is operating when act II begins. Célimène immediately observes that Alceste has brought her home only to pick a fight: "C'est pour me quereller donc, à ce que je vois, / Que vous avez voulu me ramener chez moi?" (II, i, 455–56). He vows he will break with her, as though they were engaged, unless she discourages the admirers he condemns: "il faudra que nous rompions ensemble"; "tôt ou tard nous romprons indubitablement" (450, 452). Alceste intends to gain advantage with Célimène by threatening to leave. But a coquette measures her worth in the quantity, not the quality, of her suitors. Rather than dismiss her following she would lose one man, even one with more merit than all her other suitors combined. She is insensitive to the notion of value that Alceste raises in his full-length portrait of Clitandre, the first in the play and a foretaste of the portraits by Célimène that Alceste condemns later in the act. He asserts that her petty noble suitors are worthless. This quarrel with Célimène runs parallel to the first-act argument with Philinte: mistress, like friend, is reproached a willingness to embrace and attend to nonentities instead of concentrating exclusively on the unique man of value. In act I Alceste had tried to embarrass Philinte by mimicking his greeting of the unknown person; in act II he imitates Clitandre to shame Célimène. By making her laugh at his rival, he can acquire advantage over Clitandre (standing in for all the rivals) and Célimène.

> Mais au moins dites-moi, madame, par quel sort
> Votre Clitandre a l'heur de vous plaire si fort.
> Sur quel fonds de mérite et de vertu sublime
> Appuyez-vous en lui l'honneur de votre estime?
> Est-ce par l'ongle long qu'il porte au petit doigt
> Qu'il s'est acquis chez vous l'estime où l'on le voit?
> Vous êtes-vous rendue, avec tout le beau monde,
> Au mérite éclatant de sa perruque blonde?
> Sont-ce ses grands canons qui vous le font aimer?
> L'amas de ses rubans a-t-il su vous charmer?
> Est-ce par les appas de sa vaste rhingrave
> Qu'il a gagné votre âme, en faisant votre esclave?
> Ou sa façon de rire et son ton de fausset
> Ont-ils de vous toucher su trouver le secret?
>
> (475–88)

Alceste's distinction of inherent deep merit from superficial signs of value touches the ethical node of the comedy. He mockingly links the "fonds de mérite et de vertu sublime" to the "mérite éclatant" of wigs, clothing, and affected behavior. (The audience may recall that Oronte had applied to Alceste the phrase "mérite éclatant" in a context rendering it paradoxical.) Alceste fails to subdue Célimène, however, for, like Philinte, she cites obligation—as a function of self-interest—as reason for receiving Clitandre. In absolute terms the suitors may be worthless, but they exert influence. Alceste demands that Célimène lose her lawsuit, dismiss her suitors, and, in effect, undergo public humiliation. Is this so that he may be acknowledged as the source of all her value as he "raises" her before witnesses? (To anticipate: at the end when she is humiliated, he does not in fact rescue her. But then no witnesses close to the court remain to see his merit as the pardoning imitator or rival of the king; the only ones left are the independent Éliante and Philinte.) "Perdez votre procès, madame, avec constance, / Et ne ménagez point un rival qui m'offense" (493–94). Alceste pits his own importance against the lawsuit, expecting Célimène to choose a reduction to nullity so he may endow her with his value, the existence of which remains unproven. He asks her to take a tremendous risk. This relationship will become more explicit in act IV; here it is implicit in the advice to banish Clitandre and lose the case. In proof of her love Célimène must sacrifice material well-being, ego, the attentions of influential admirers—all to give Alceste advantage. Her statement that he possesses, as the rivals do not, "le bonheur de savoir que vous êtes aimé" (503) leaves him unsatisfied and more demanding: "Et quel lieu de le croire a mon coeur enflammé?" (504). The favoritism he requests does not involve sexual acts (as Arsinoé insinuates in act III), but the definitive rejection of the influential courtiers in terms of whose attentions Célimène's standing is measurable. His advantage paradoxically would flow from the renunciation of hers. But Alceste does not love her for any intrinsic merit, either, that would be left after the suitors were banished; as he explicitly states in act IV and as he suggests here—"Personne n'a, madame, aimé comme je fais" (524)—he considers her as a woman esthetically beautiful whom he intends to infuse with ethical value. The trouble is that his ethical value and program remain problematic in nature and undefined through actions.

Acaste's imminent arrival interrupts the dispute; but Molière has Alceste and Célimène repeat its terms in a concentrated passage. The parallelism with Alceste's earlier quarrel with Philinte extends to the repetition of the offending act. The announcement of Acaste's entrance provokes Alceste to reiterate his objections and Célimène to defend her self-interest: "C'est un homme à jamais ne me le pardonner, / S'il savait que sa vue eût pu m'importuner" (539–40). She will not risk the humiliating damage Acaste might work, even though she may agree with Alceste about him. But, with the marquis about to appear, Célimène cannot risk Alceste's obstreperous behavior either, and she may agree with him to prevent him from making a scene:

> Mon Dieu! de ses pareils la bienveillance importe,
> Et ce sont de ces gens qui, je ne sais comment,
> Ont gagné dans la cour de parler hautement.
> Dans tous les entretiens on les voit s'introduire;
> Ils ne sauraient servir, mais ils peuvent nous nuire,
> Et jamais, quelque appui qu'on puisse avoir ailleurs,
> On ne doit se brouiller avec ces grands brailleurs.
>
> (542–48)

In any event, Molière is setting an ideological framework concerning the court that is the context for the ensuing portrait scene.

Célimène's satirical portrait gallery, II, iv, is framed by references to the milieu where her subjects thrive: the court, from which Clitandre has come—"Parbleu! je viens du Louvre . . . au levé" (568)—and to which he will return—"Moi, pourvu que je puisse être au petit couché, / Je n'ai point d'autre affaire où je sois attaché" (739–40). These allusions identify the rank enjoyed by the salon's members; and the audience may be surprised to learn that the king favors these people with attendance at intimate ceremonies. Oronte did not seem instantly so foolish as Clitandre; but the audience was not prepared to side with Alceste against Oronte as it is ready to judge Clitandre. Alceste has just described him, accurately according to the costume now seen and perhaps just as precisely regarding his inherent worth. The audience may agree with Alceste about Clitandre and, by extension and association, Acaste.

Molière's strategy here is perilous, if the audience does share Alceste's opinion. His devaluing, malicious portrait of Clitandre is meant to shame Célimène into dropping him as a suitor. The audience, unconcerned with Clitandre as a rival for Célimène's love, cannot share Alceste's motive. But it can question the justice governing the king's awarding of favor to such as Clitandre (or the justice presiding over rank assigned at birth, Fortune). That snare Molière must avoid: if we allow ourselves to agree with Alceste over Clitandre's nullity, covered by unusual dress and speech, then we may sympathize with him concerning the justice that admits Clitandre to royal ceremonies, and consequently imitate Alceste's incorrect representation of justice. We are prepared to grant certain specifics: the marquis are fools, Oronte is no great poet, Célimène has faults; but Alceste's behavior must prevent our agreement on the question of just and unjust behavior. The arrangement of episodes and the intrusion of surprising or incoherent elements, like Éliante's speech in praise of lovers, will serve as reminders that Alceste's notions of justice are applicable neither to court nor salon.

Nobles at the real court competed for honors. They had rank through birthright—or through the purchase of *charges*, positions in royal service—and they attracted the king's attention in genuine service, which was primarily military for the traditional nobility as opposed to the marquis, who recently had acquired title. Molière's marquis are not satirical portraits of real courtiers (certain aristocrats were, however, identified with Alceste, and it takes only a little imagination to compare him with the disillusioned La Rochefoucauld). Although they are not *caractères* meant to condemn the *moeurs de ce siècle*, they do point to the true nobility's need to attract royal attention, demonstrate inherent merit—or difference—and receive rewards. Molière's petits marquis and Alceste behave absurdly because they misinterpret the nature of favor. The only adequate solution to the problem is a secular counterpart to the Christian baroque doctrine shaping *Don Quixote*, *La Vida es sueño*, and Pascal's wager: *honnêteté* is its own reward, for it produces the ethical life of good works. The rest follows of itself: the king will recognize merit and will reward according to his free grace; and should he not, that does not matter to the man for whom ethical attitudes and works provide happiness.

Célimène's portraits present members of the fictional court as reduced to the level of a series of mechanical devices that grab attention in order to grasp advantage. Her subjects miss the point that favor depends on the king's or lover's or God's inexplicable choice. The audience finds pertinent Alceste's objection that the marquis, who behave with similar gimmickry, greet with feigned respect and love the people whom they mock:

> Cependant aucun d'eux à vos yeux ne se montre
> Qu'on ne vous voie en hâte aller à sa rencontre,
> Lui présenter la main et d'un baiser flatteur
> Appuyer les serments d'être son serviteur.

(653–56)

Alceste notices the disparity between the marquis' sense of their friends' nullity and the respect they show for signs of value that the others assume. Such acknowledgment holds in a tense equilibrium both court and salon. Arsinoé and Célimène act out the destructive impulse to upset the balance in III, iii; so does Oronte in his campaign against Alceste, referred to at V, i, 1505–16.

The portraits perform such a destructive service, or disservice, without, however, harming those who are exposed. No one loses favor as a consequence. The portraits are verbal gestures with as little real substance as the subjects they disparage. Malicious but harmless caricatures reassure Célimène's guests of their advantage by ridiculing *in absentia* the rival seekers after favor at court. People here seem to believe that the pool of royal favor is limited. They do not realize the futility of disparaging rivals, even of being rivals at court, since the king, like God, disposes of limitless stores of grace and is not unduly influenced by shows of merit, particularly where intrinsic value is absent. The same misunderstanding persists in the salon, where rivals vie for Célimène's favor. But, unlike the king who can love his entire court and the kingdom, she loves no one. Her portraits in this scene and in the letters read in act V ignore whatever virtues her subjects possess, and she is incapable of overlooking faults, minor and major, as a true lover does. Nor does Alceste come to the defense of her victims. He remains silent in his corner. His stance, isolated and ignoring, characteristically suggests that the others are not worth his attention; he might, however, simply be waiting for the session to run its course, so he may continue the interrupted inquisition of Célimène after the marquis leave.

But, despite himself, he is finally drawn into the conversation—
which becomes a quarrel—when a portrait bears his likeness. He
appears detached until his own virtue, or his own means of gaining
advantage, is questioned.

Célimène succinctly identifies Damis as a friend when Philinte
proposes him as a subject (631–32). But, encouraged or provoked,
she will for applause find fault with him. The sequence leading to
the portrait of Damis is revealing. It involves Philinte and Éliante,
previously silent witnesses, who are not neutral characters but sensitive observers who know how to make Alceste join the group to
defend or abandon his doctrine. The sequence begins as Célimène
disparages Cléon, "chez qui vont aujourd'hui / Nos plus honnêtes
gens" (623–24), according to Clitandre. Célimène diminishes him and
the most discriminating guests to his table, saying: "Que de son
cuisinier il s'est fait un mérite, / Et que c'est à sa table à qui l'on
rend visite" (625–26). The cream of society pretends to honor Cléon's
personal value, she implies, while profiting from his method of
acquiring distinction. When some extraordinary pleasure is offered,
it is easy to overlook the position that superficial signs do not demonstrate or substitute for genuine ethical worth. The *honnêtes gens*
respect Cléon's table, not him. The audience must sympathize: it
is hard to resist an extraordinary sensual temptation, like a meal or
an exceptional, although perhaps ethically worthless, person—
which is Alceste's situation with respect to Célimène. In this concise
portrait Molière evokes a bond between Cléon's guests and the audience: we all compromise absolute—dogmatic—values for rare
pleasures, and we may discover that the purveyors of such experiences have qualities, previously unsuspected on account of our snob-
bery, that are worthy of respect; we may go for dinner and return
for the person's own merits. Célimène implies that such is impossible; but our experience may find her wrong, even as we acknowledge that people wittingly take advantage of available pleasures belonging to sophisticated civilization, like stylish clothing, manners,
literature. Paradoxically, we may decry Cléon and take his meal,
just as Célimène ridicules Acaste in his absence and desires his

influence. Alceste may justly object to this behavior; but it is as tempting to enjoy the feast as to cultivate the purveyors of power. Célimène's couplet about Cléon's table prompts Éliante to break her silence. (She had spoken an aside to Philinte at 583–84 but had not joined the general conversation.) "Il prend soin d'y servir des mets fort délicats" (627), she says, explaining why people visit Cléon, but also seeming to prompt Célimène to continue. Three verses of satire result: "Oui, mais je voudrais bien qu'il ne s'y servît pas; / C'est un fort méchant plat que sa sotte personne, / Et qui gâte, à mon goût, tous les repas qu'il donne" (628–30). Philinte, in his turn, asks for an opinion of Cléon's uncle Damis. He may expect Célimène to expose a certain fault, since all the members of this limited society know one another. Célimène's response, in its brevity, recalls that concerning Cléon, but not in its surprising point: "Il est de mes amis" (632). Might friendship keep Célimène from an attack? Philinte's interjection, "Je le trouve honnête homme et d'un air assez sage" (633), like Éliante's remark, launches Célimène into a longer portrait that resembles Alceste— the reason, perhaps, she had tactfully not caricatured Damis immediately. She might be alluding to Alceste's behavior over Oronte's sonnet when she says: "Il veut voir des défauts à tout ce qu'on écrit" (639); and Alceste, like Damis, "se met au-dessus de tous les autres gens" (644). As for the last four verses:

Aux conversations même il trouve à reprendre,
Ce sont propos trop bas pour y daigner descendre,
Et, les deux bras croisés, du haut de son esprit,
Il regarde en pitié tout ce que chacun dit.

(645–48)

there is Alceste standing apart, arms crossed, disdaining the conversation. Because Célimène's caricature of her "ami" Damis fits Alceste, she has broken a cardinal rule of salon and court by diminishing to appearances someone actually present. To defend himself, Alceste violates it too, counterattacking the petits marquis whom he also calls "friends," although sarcastically: "mes bons amis

95

de cour" (651). Célimène breaks a convention, Alceste follows suit, and destruction threatens the salon.

"Friends" at court, Alceste observes, embrace and offer services as strategies of advantage.

> Allons, ferme, poussez, mes bons amis de cour!
> Vous n'en épargnez point, et chacun a son tour.
> Cependant aucun d'eux à vos yeux ne se montre
> Qu'on ne vous voie en hâte aller à sa rencontre,
> Lui présenter la main et d'un baiser flatteur
> Appuyer les serments d'être son serviteur.
>
> (651–56)

The counterattack, accompanied by exaggerated gestures, should divert attention from his own caricature. But the maneuver backfires. Célimène does not resist rising to the bait of another provocative remark by Philinte (667–68); she portrays Alceste openly as the spirit of contradiction. An argument ensues amongst her suitors concerning Célimène's faults. Order has broken down in the salon.

Alceste counterattacks to rid the salon of rivals by generating unpleasantness. He had ordered Célimène to renounce them, and he had quarreled as they entered. Now he announces that he would banish,

> . . . moi, tous ces lâches amants
> Que je verrais soumis à tous mes sentiments,
> Et dont, à tout propos, les molles complaisances
> Donneraient de l'encens à mes extravagances.
>
> (703–6)

Something very funny operates here: Alceste repeats what Célimène has done to him, imitating her as in a portrait but with a twist; his version of Célimène inaccurately represents her in "*mes* sentiments" and "*mes* extravagances." The particularly funny conclusion ascribes "extravagances" to Célimène; but Alceste is the extravagant here, especially as his gestures sweeping away the rivals, another antiembracing movement, increase the comedy.

Célimène prolongs the quarrel with a caricature of Alceste's proposal. She apparently does not recognize the danger threatening her salon. Éliante, however, does. Her great speech (II, iv, 711–30), drawing upon Lucretius' *De rerum natura* (book 4, 1149–65), intervenes like an aria, different in manner and content from the preceding exchanges, as her explanation of lovers' behavior contradicts the views of Alceste and his rivals. A lover, she says, knows how to interpret a beloved's shortcomings as virtues inspiring admiration. Such deliberate misreading should qualify him as "comic." He acts unreasonably—unless he follows some order known only to the heart.

Nor does the lover apparently behave justly; his charity, however, relates him to the ethics of the Lucretian poem inspiring the passage. For dramaturgical reasons, Molière must have intended to stop the show with Éliante's speech: the argument among the other characters could go no further without destroying the salon. He must also have had reasons of substance. Éliante's meaning conforms to the ethical structure governing justice at the court, for the lover's charity resembles the king's grace (and God's mercy). Lucretius' account of the origin of human values is in accord with not only Éliante's views but the analogous systems of royal and divine justice as well. Molière has inserted what amounts to an Epicurean, thus *libertin* document— but it could also be called "humanist"—that complements and clarifies the royalist and Christian ideologies (or mythologies) on which the comedy is constructed.

Lucretius' Epicurean philosophy deals with the ethics of human behavior against a background of physics. He sets man in a world still fraught with catastrophe, as Nature wears out and as the atoms move without any intelligence guiding them. The universe came into existence by chance; apparent order emerged from chaos by chance; and the world will disintegrate the same way. His poem ends narrating a final cataclysm. Against this purposeless background man must act differently although, as a part of Nature, he too resists physiological and psychological control: the chance swerving of atoms affects his emotions and passions as it produces calamities in Nature. In the Epicurean scheme, man must escape universal disorder and his own chaos to live blissfully like the "gods," archetypal, ideal, fictional beings created by the poetic imagination. Man can resemble an idea of godliness by his behavior and the invention of values that permit the imposition of order upon himself. Just as man tries to subjugate Nature for his advantage, he must impose order on himself through a science of ethics which assigns values to modes of behavior despite the accidentals characteristic of Nature. Unstable Nature threatens to collapse; but human values are permanent, and ethics denote man's differences from the natural world that gives him birth and reclaims him in death. Epicurus' philosophy stresses human dignity and encourages man to control, even to reform human nature through conscious purpose in opposition to Nature, and to establish values free of the disintegration to which the natural world is subject. (Corneille's Auguste, that epitome of the baroque hero, is an Epicurean *sans le savoir*.)

Éliante's speech reflects these Lucretian ethics. A lover chooses to assign values in poetic terms to physical, accidental qualities. He imposes order on things arranged by chance, and he confers value so the beloved may behave as if she had the virtue he attributes to her. Her value exists relative to the lover's wish to discover qualities releasing her from vagaries of fortune. Éliante's speech may be satirical—Lucretius can be ironic, too—and in context her speech may seem funny. Only lovers can readily accept her idea. Her depiction of love, as an alternative to Alceste's and the marquis' views, is hard to take. She may even seem to be putting herself on display with a showpiece permitting her to shine as brilliantly as Célimène. What passes unobserved, however, is that the philosophy enacted by her poetical lovers is exactly what this salon needs to keep it from imminent chaos. An audience knowing Lucretius might grasp the speech's wider implications; but most audiences cannot accept as a model the attitudes she enunciates. Nevertheless, her speech is the ideological heart of the play, set off by its dramatic context. That the ideology passes unnoticed in its quasi-satiric form indicates the characters'—and our own—unreadiness to recognize the propositions that merit and advantage exist as relative realities because of some loving bestower, and that no individual may justifiably boast of his advantages. We react to the speech as the characters do: Molière's strategy again duplicates responses on stage and in the theater audience. Later reflection may suggest that a solution to the play's ethical problems was at hand in act II. Such second-guessing corresponds to enlightenment concerning moral dilemmas in our own experience when it is too late.

Alceste certainly misses the point. He immediately sets out to contradict Éliante: "Et moi, je soutiens, moi . . ." (731). He may not even have been listening: his posture would indicate that. He means to resume the argument. To cut him off, Célimène proposes a stroll. Alceste correctly surmises she wants to get rid of him and boorishly tries to embarrass her. The scene ends as it began. When the marquis entered, they heard Alceste insist that Célimène choose one suitor. At the end of the scene he maintains that he will outstay his rivals to complete the tête-à-tête with Célimène. Her response, "C'est pour rire, je crois" (741), resembles her earlier reply, "Vous vous moquez, je pense" (566). Once again, an intrusion of the court saves her, in the person this time of the marshals' guard.

Reminders of the court follow Éliante's speech, in Clitandre's remark about the *petit coucher* and the guard's arrival. The value of the members of the court has been questioned implicitly and explicitly in the portrait scene. One may wonder whether these people at whom we have laughed do not resemble beloveds as described by Éliante: do the marquis enjoy high station at court, despite their failings and lack of worth, through some action or attitude of the king like the lover's? The king is surely less absolute than Alceste; does he know how to assign value where, to all appearances, it is missing? The court is governed by manners that impose order, control the nobility, and prevent chaos. Like the lover, does the king gain advantage by guaranteeing the hierarchy over which he presides? Grace produces order and promotes civilization, both of which are missing from Célimène's salon as act II ends. In act III it becomes clear why love is also absent.

The scene between Acaste and Clitandre (III, i) makes apparent a crucial distinction between court and salon while it develops the theme of friendship in perverse forms that the later dialogue of Célimène and Arsinoé extends. Alceste is away when act III begins, a change in construction from the preceding acts. He has been summoned to be reconciled with Oronte by the court's authority so that the rivals' "friendship" may be patched up for appearances' sake. Meanwhile in the salon the behavior of two presumed friends betrays their bond without their noticing it. They may be friends at court where they take their share, more or less equal, of the king's infinite bounties. Célimène, however, may favor only one man. The desire to appear uniquely worthy of her rewards undoes the ties of friendship. No rival here shrinks from humiliating the others to gain access to her. Acaste and Clitandre substantiate Alceste's charge: social behavior does cover the falsity of valueless people who have no love. Their protestations of devotion and their embraces while they strike their bargain reflect a perversion of the love that, within a Christian ideology, is supposed to bind up society in fellowship. Acaste's boasts indicate his sense of civilization (III, i, 781–804); but his readiness to humiliate Clitandre suggests that his ethics belong to the jungle. Hobbes and Pascal are corroborated, for the civil agreements struck in Célimène's salon reveal savage egoism. The social contract perpetrates myths to maintain an artificial order where man's wants can be satisfied. But culture does not necessarily denote altruism; civilized man may sacrifice his fellows to his own interests, as in the state of nature. Substituting one myth, civilization, does not redeem man from the effects of another myth, the Fall, while in a comic, nonheroic vision the Christian ideology of charity is apt to be ignored or followed perversely rather than faithfully. Alceste's invectives against humanity (I, i, 87–96, 118–44) are of a piece with Christian condemnation, without, however, any counterpoise of redemption. He threatens to leave civilization and corrupt, fallen man; but it is doubtful that he will find in his déserts another kind of man approximating an ideal out of some golden age.

Molière draws on such a vision in *La Princesse d'Élide* and *Les Amants magnifiques*, in which, as in *Le Misanthrope*, rival suitors and courtiers vie for one beautiful and gifted woman, while a royal court's civilization is mingled with pastoral and a non-Christian, pseudo-pagan mythology. Poetry dwelling on golden ages depends on the convention that the Fall left the idealized characters untouched; the reader, or audience, suspends belief that man has sinned and that Nature no longer bountifully satisfies all his wants. (The satyrs are intruders in the pastoral's perfection. Their brutality is a reminder of the postlapsarian state from which the idealized humans, but not the reader, are exempt.) Even the rivals for the single beloved behave nobly. The pastoral's characters are courtly without a court, with Nature itself taking the part of the royal authority; and, confident in Nature and free from preoccupation with their merits, the characters do not seek advantage. Alceste should flee to such a world. That kind of place, however, is not found even in Molière's pastorals, where the vision is mixed: rivals there do strive to gain advantage, and they are not friendly, especially with the outstanding suitor who lacks rank through birthright. Neither Alceste nor Molière's characters in the courtly spectacles can ignore the fact of fallen human nature, of which the marquis' conversation provides ample proof.

Their friendship is undermined by their boasting. Each one agrees to withdraw as a suitor, should proof of Célimène's favor to his rival be shown. No risk is involved, and neither expects to lose. These men look forward to humiliating their rival—their friend—just as they delight in Célimène's satirical portraits. A genuine friend would find value in abnegation and the fact that a friend won the coveted prize. The comedy here lies in the wrongness of their agreement, understood against such an ideal of friendship, and in an ironic twist: while their friendship is revealed as worthless, Célimène loves neither, and she too lacks ethical value, for she has misled her suitors with pleasing but empty promises of favor. The marquis' riskless wager can produce no gain. But they are unconcerned by the precariousness of their relationship when they laughingly leave the known enemies Célimène and Arsinoé to protest their mutual affection.

That conversation develops more openly the nature of such civilized friendships. No love is lost between these women, as Célimène makes clear before Arsinoé enters. And their rivalry for Alceste is as contrived as the friendship they proclaim as they embrace. Neither loves Alceste: nothing suggests that either woman considers him except as a man to be kept as a suitor or to be stolen in order to detract from her rival's worth measured in the number of men courting her. Molière could have let Célimène declare her love for Alceste to Éliante, if he had wanted the audience to perceive it as real: such a confession exists at the very beginning of *Dom Garcie de Navarre*, from which Molière transferred passages to *Le Misanthrope*. But Célimène just keeps Alceste dangling like Oronte, Acaste, and Clitandre. For a coquette, numbers determine value, and keeping a crowd around precludes the commitment that makes a coquette an ordinary woman again. That crowd makes Arsinoé jealous; stealing Alceste would diminish Célimène within her own false reasoning.

Alceste is like a pawn in a competition for his attention: he is not loved for intrinsic merit or some *je ne sais quoi*. (Arsinoé cannot appreciate his sincerity, for she would be among his first victims.) This attitude corresponds to the men's reasoning, as they court Célimène to be able to boast of her favors as a visible sign of their worth: possessing or just being the favorite of this attractive woman would connote extraordinary advantage and value. According to the marquis's claim that Célimène is flawless (II, iv, 695–98), she is the paragon of women who will reward the paragon of men, as though she were like the perfect king or God who, the marquis might speciously reason, recognizes and rewards intrinsic worth. The men use Célimène, "deified" and "reified" at the same time, as a means to their advantage and not just to erotic ends. Arsinoé's innuendoes that Célimène rewards her suitors with sexual favors are misleading (III, iv, 1001–16). The men may desire her physically, but that is secondary.

If Célimène and Arsinoé are sexually attracted to Alceste, that too is of minimal importance. Their rivalry provokes them, like the marquis, to declare their friendship, and they insult each other in a context of friendly advice and persuasion that recalls Alceste's tactic with Oronte. Arsinoé slanders Célimène to her face (III, iv, 878–912) by recounting the comments of "gens de vertu singulière" (885), which are as transparently fictitious as Alceste's conversation with a would-be poet. Her imputation of the criticism to other people—"Non que j'y croie, au fond, l'honnêteté blessée" (905)—makes Célimène seem an object of public derision. To humiliate Célimène, Arsinoé invokes her obligation to correct her friend and inform her of public opinion (in a manner reminiscent of Alceste's own program). Arsinoé abuses the structures of friendship and guest relationships, which she treats contemptuously. (She deserves her ensuing comeuppance in kind, which pleases the audience.) Arsinoé's scorn of civil conventions is immediately apparent as she refuses Célimène's invitation to sit (878): "Il n'est pas nécessaire, / Madame" (878–79); she ignores a minimal gesture of hospitality while preserving her advantage intact and undiluted by Célimène's least service. The polite "Madames" the women exchange emphasize Arsinoé's rudeness; and the pairing of civility and rudeness brings out her perverse use of friendship as a specious isotype of the dialectic of obligation.

So does Célimène's reply, a faithful reflection of Arsinoé's strategy; by parody, a comic technique of imitation for purposes of denigration, she exposes Arsinoé's perversion of amicable conduct. Célimène's presentation of *her* recent conversation about Arsinoé's morals is an imitation of a parodic imitation of behavior between friends, like that of the marquis. Célimène has not missed her visitor's malice. The parody in return demeans Arsinoé—a classic example of the perverse imitator beaten at her own game. Célimène grinds in the humiliation of the parody by citing Arsinoé verbatim in conclusion:

Madame, je vous crois aussi trop raisonnable
Pour ne pas prendre bien cet avis profitable,
Et pour l'attribuer qu'aux mouvements secrets
D'un zèle qui m'attache à tous vos intérêts.

(957–60)

The prude's strategy is exposed and the coquette is on the counteroffensive. Now a direct confrontation follows on the subject of the earlier dialogue between the rival suitors: advantage and merit. To Célimène's claims that youth and charm attract suitors (975–84, 991–1000), Arsinoé replies that she is not much older than her friend (985–90); and she insinuates that Célimène's charm takes the form of sexual favors (1001–24). She finally states in her own voice the charges of immorality that she had earlier attributed to "gens de bien"; by questioning Célimène's worth, she also makes explicit again the subject of individual value, whose absence can be disguised by manipulating accidentals and exhibiting whatever titillates men who care more for pleasure than for inherent merit. The audience does wonder why Célimène is courted so assiduously by suitors who all, except Alceste, seem confident of conquest; has any of them been rewarded sexually? Arsinoé's inferences add to our doubts, which resemble Alceste's: this sequence of scenes into which Alceste will enter establishes a common attitude we share with him concerning Célimène. We too want to learn which rival she favors—in a sense that is the plot of the play—and whether she has bestowed preference in some erotic manner. The possibility that Célimène has committed herself sexually may embarrass us and offend our conventions—*bienséances* influence real life as well as the behavior and language of the stage. Alceste faces that question by demanding proof, in the expulsion of the other suitors, that she prefers him; he would rather ignore the other possibility and he does not accept joyously Arsinoé's offer to establish proof of Célimène's infidelity. Although Célimène parries them, Arsinoé's charges increase our uneasiness by sheer repetition of a vocabulary juxtaposing "mérite" and sexual implications in the only passage which alludes overtly and continuously to erotic activity:

> Hélas! et croyez-vous que l'on se mette en peine
> De ce nombre d'amants dont vous faites la vaine?
> Et qu'il ne nous soit pas fort aisé de juger
> À quel prix aujourd'hui l'on peut les engager?

Pensez-vous faire croire, à voir comme tout roule,
Que votre seul mérite attire cette foule?
Qu'ils ne brûlent pour vous que d'un honnête amour,
Et que pour vos vertus ils vous font tous la cour?
On ne s'aveugle point par de vaines défaites,
Le monde n'est point dupe, et j'en vois qui sont faites
À pouvoir inspirer de tendres sentiments,
Qui chez elles pourtant ne fixent point d'amants;
Et de là nous pouvons tirer des conséquences,
Qu'on n'acquiert point leurs coeurs sans de grandes avances,
Qu'aucun pour nos beaux yeux n'est notre soupirant,
Et qu'il faut acheter tous les soins qu'on nous rend.
Ne vous enflez donc point d'une si grande gloire
Pour les petits brillants d'une faible victoire,
Et corrigez un peu l'orgueil de vos appas
De traiter pour cela les gens de haut en bas.
Si nos yeux enviaient les conquêtes des vôtres,
Je pense qu'on pourrait faire comme les autres,
Ne se point ménager, et vous faire bien voir
Que l'on a des amants quand on en veut avoir.

(1001–24)

Eight specific references to sexual favors and desires occur in twenty-four verses. Easy access now determines a coquette's "value." (Arsinoé, it will turn out, is not entirely wrong—except that we never learn whether Célimène delivers on promises to her suitors.) The scene ends without an embrace, like the one with which Acaste and Clitandre may have sealed their agreement. The pretense of friendly service vanishes. Arsinoé has come to humiliate Célimène with a perversion of friendship, then by open attacks on the source of Célimène's pride, the number of her admirers. Célimène nevertheless gains a triumph, and Arsinoé cuts short the talk as rudely as she had begun it:

. . . Brisons, madame, un pareil entretien,
Il pousserait trop loin votre esprit et le mien;
Et j'aurais pris déjà le congé qu'il faut prendre,
Si mon carrosse encor ne m'obligeait d'attendre.

(1027–30)

Alceste's arrival permits Célimène an exit that is more gracious than Arsinoé's remark. She can still satisfy a hostess' duty to entertain a guest; she maintains advantage even while flaunting confidence in her power over Alceste. Leaving him with a jealous rival virtually constitutes an act of provocation in the guise of a hostess' best manners.

Alceste enters subdued. He says nothing to Célimène and does not object to being left with Arsinoé, even though he has presumably come to tell of his forced reconciliation with Oronte—and to receive consolation. He gets the opposite, for Arsinoé reminds him that the court does not reward his deserts and she accuses Célimène of betraying him. In context, her proposals seem calculated to steal him from the rival who has just humiliated her, not to express love. She dwells on Alceste's worth in a way recalling her insistence on Célimène's proferring of sexual favors. The word "mérite" recurs in her speeches, and his responses:

> En vérité, les gens d'un mérite sublime
> Entraînent de chacun et l'amour et l'estime,
> Et le vôtre sans doute a des charmes secrets
> Qui font entrer mon coeur dans tous vos intérêts.
>
> (1045–48)

> Et le mérite enfin que vous nous faites voir
>
> (1060)

> Un mérite éclatant se déterre lui-même;
> Du vôtre, en bien des lieux, on fait un cas extrême,
> Et vous saurez de moi qu'en deux fort bons endroits
> Vous fûtes hier loué par des gens d'un grand poids.
>
> (1065–68)

Arsinoé again reports probably fictitious conversations, not to disparage but to praise Alceste. He responds mildly, not troubling to challenge her. He would discourage her and be left alone: he has performed no distinguished service to demonstrate his worth. The audience, aware that Alceste does not believe he must accomplish such deeds, recognizes that he is trying to get rid of Arsinoé when he claims that the court does not care about value. Besides,

> . . . l'on loue aujourd'hui tout le monde,
> Et le siècle par là n'a rien qu'on ne confonde;
> Tout est d'un grand mérite également doué,
> Ce n'est plus un honneur que de se voir loué;
> D'éloges on regorge, à la tête on les jette,
> Et mon valet de chambre est mis dans la Gazette.
>
> (1069–74)

Alceste's joke about his servant distracts from the serious question of obligation to Arsinoé for her services. Like Oronte, she touches on the issue that depresses Alceste: owing status to other people's intervention instead of being recognized for one's inherent merit and enjoying rank free of any obligation. An offer of service creates debts that Alceste will not honor, particularly since Arsinoé must construe them as redeemable in sex and love. Her offer, the audience realizes, is meant to humiliate Célimène rather than to dignify Alceste. This motive underlies the shift in topic to Alceste's unfortunate choice of a mistress. Since he is not enticed by her service at court, Arsinoé offers information exposing Célimène's infidelity. Alceste observes that she is betraying a friend (1103–6). Friendship and charity, cited as reasons for informing Alceste—"L'état où je vous vois afflige trop mon âme" (1109)—disguise advantage and obligation, as Alceste's ironic response indicates: "de pareils avis obligent un amant" (1112). Arsinoé's "charité se serait bien passée / De jeter dans le mien [mon coeur] une telle pensée" (1117–18). Arsinoé pretends to do Alceste a favor in order to do Célimène dirt; and she intends to obligate, not to oblige, Alceste with self-interested "charity" that will humiliate her rival and embarrass Alceste. He had wanted proof of Célimène's preference; he will obtain a "preuve fidèle / De l'infidélité" (1129–30) of Célimène's heart, in the name of charity, friendship, and Arsinoé's recognition of Alceste's superior worth.

All of act III deals with perverse notions of friendship and with disobliging behavior in the guise of civil or charitable actions committed as "service." In this place without love, all the manifestations of civility and friendship resound with what Pascal called the hollowness of the human heart.

At the beginning of act IV, the generosity of Éliante and Philinte provides a counterpoise to the salon's malice and emptiness. Their meeting, as close to a love scene as Molière allows in the play, separates Arsinoé's betrayal of her "friend" and Alceste's ravings over Célimène's alleged infidelities. Alceste's interruption to offer himself to Éliante is an unwitting parody or perversion of a genuine love scene. The sequence starts with Philinte's narration, with mimetic gestures, of Alceste's behavior at the marshals' court, thus extending into act IV the preceding act's preoccupation with false friendship. Alceste agreed that Oronte was a "galant homme en toutes les manières, / Homme de qualité, de mérite et de coeur" (IV, i, 1146–47), but declared that such qualities did not guarantee that he could write decent poetry. Alceste's formulaic apology indicates empty friendship: "Monsieur, je suis fâché d'être si difficile; / Et, pour l'amour de vous, je voudrais de bon coeur / Avoir trouvé tantôt votre sonnet meilleur" (1158–60).

The king's court of justice forces Alceste to submit lest he suffer the public humiliation of banishment from the royal court: leaving voluntarily and exclusion are not the same. And Alceste may still find consolation in the salon, where he plans to exclude his rivals and impose his own justice. Philinte's questions about Alceste's chances with Célimène remind the audience of those intentions and suggest that Alceste may find humiliation in the salon too. In effect, a parity or structural analogy exists between court and salon, and between the kinds of justice operative in them.

Justice cannot exist in the absence of genuine friendship and love. The marshals' justice induces no love between Alceste and Oronte, whose embrace is supposed to stifle their discord: "Et dans une embrassade, on leur a, pour conclure, / Fait vite envelopper toute la procédure" (1161–62). A forced embrace is a false image of a gesture signifying love and the mutual forgiveness of human weakness; it is a simulacrum lacking substance because the participants' frailty, their human nature, denies them the ability to pardon, and because their rivalry in the salon leading to the boudoir, as in the court leading to the king's chamber, prevents them from exercising generosity. If only they could admit how little value Célimène has; if only they realized that an example of ethical behavior might infuse her with value. But the false embrace is a virtual model for false pardon, without the ethical concomitant of conversion. Their embrace should be an act denoting the heroic ideal of generosity in imitation of the king represented by the marshals. It is instead an exercise in esthetics with no ethical substance.

Éliante reacts to the narration according to her feeling for Alceste. Unlike the audience, she does not laugh at an episode which is comic—because the concluding embrace imitates perversely an archetypal action of friendship and forgiveness—and funny because of Alceste's typical, exaggerated language. Éliante responds like a Lucretian lover, interpreting as virtue what others find defective. She considers Alceste's unusual behavior exceptional, his sincerity noble and heroic.

> Dans ses façons d'agir il est fort singulier,
> Mais j'en fais, je l'avoue, un cas particulier,
> Et la sincérité dont son âme se pîque
> A quelque chose en soi de noble et d'héroïque.
> C'est une vertu rare au siècle d'aujourd'hui,
> Et je la voudrais voir partout comme chez lui.
>
> (1163–68)

The audience makes no exceptions for Alceste and cannot admire his "sincerity" for he has capitulated to the marshals' power while failing to pardon Oronte's all-too-human desire to appear brilliant despite his limitations. Éliante demonstrates love's power to stimulate generosity, even to the point of error, *if it is possible to be wrong in exercising charity.*

Éliante also speaks generously of her cousin. She does not censure Célimène for encouraging many suitors: "Son coeur de ce qu'il sent n'est pas bien sûr lui-même; / Il aime quelquefois sans qu'il le sache bien, / Et croit aimer aussi parfois qu'il n'en est rien" (1182–84). Her nobility is most apparent, however, in her willingness to let Célimène have Alceste, whom Éliante herself loves. Above all she desires his satisfaction: "si c'était qu'à moi la chose pût tenir, / Moi-même à ce qu'il aime on me verrait l'unir" (1195–96). If Célimène does not reward his devotion, Éliante will gladly marry Alceste. Éliante and Philinte reach an agreement here that stands in opposition to the marquis' bargain. Each states support for Alceste's courtship, effacing himself before a rival who is, primarily, a friend. Philinte presents himself as Éliante's suitor only if Alceste, married to Célimène, is no longer free. He accepts Éliante's preference for Alceste and does not seek advantage over his friend by the means typical of the salon, character assassination and boasting. That generosity inspires Éliante to consider Philinte's suit seriously: self-effacement, lack of egotism, devotion to a friend all demonstrate ethical merit. The audience now recognizes this fact, particularly because of the difference between this conversation and those in act III. The audience's reaction to Philinte explicitly resembles Éliante's. Her surprised reply, "Vous vous divertissez, Philinte" (1213), suggests that Philinte has not raised the subject of marriage before, out of deference to his friend's possible proposal to Éliante; she must consider herself a woman who can be interested, unlike Célimène, in only one man. Suddenly a suitor declares himself "du meilleur de mon âme" (1214); but he will make no formal proposal until Alceste's courtship of Éliante is beyond possibility: "J'attends l'occasion de m'offrir hautement, / Et de tous mes souhaits j'en presse le moment" (1215–16).

Alceste's sudden appearance tests Éliante's generosity and capacities for self-effacement. Her new awareness of Philinte's ethical superiority, however, also supports her attempt to dissuade Alceste from rash action. The audience and she must wonder whether he is sincere and whether he has considered his behavior, for he speaks and gesticulates more wildly than before. His gestures contrast with the more subdued ones that Philinte had imitated while narrating the reconciliation scene. Alceste offers love in peculiar terms: "Vengez-moi de ce trait qui doit vous faire horreur" (IV, ii, 1251). Éliante must shrink from accepting love for a vile purpose—vengeance—inconsistent with promises of courtly service:

> C'est par là que je puis prendre vengeance d'elle,
> Et je la veux punir par les sincères voeux,
> Par le profond amour, les soins respectueux,
> Les devoirs empressés et l'assidu service
> Dont ce coeur va vous faire un ardent sacrifice.
>
> (1254–58)

Love on the rebound, violently offered, contrasts with the sincere, self-effacing emotion Philinte and Éliante have just enunciated. Alceste proposes not for Éliante's merits but for Célimène's faults.

While Alceste's protestations perversely imitate a lover's offers of service, his crudity toward Philinte makes mockery of their relationship as friends: "Ah! morbleu! mêlez-vous, monsieur, de vos affaires" (1234). Philinte's presence irritates Alceste, for he has witnessed Alceste's embarrassment before the marshals; must he now observe another humiliation? Alceste does not understand that a friend does not consider such an apology degrading and that, like the lover described by Éliante, he allows for failings. Philinte minimizes the possibility of humiliation: "Une lettre peut bien tromper par l'apparence, / Et n'est pas quelquefois si coupable qu'on pense" (1241–42). Alceste's rage shows his failure to grasp the nature of Philinte's relationship with him: "Monsieur, encor un coup, laissez-moi, s'il vous plaît, / Et ne prenez souci que de votre intérêt" (1243–44). Philinte's interest lies in reconciling Alceste and Célimène so he may marry Éliante; but the faithful friend must also keep Alceste from appearing foolish before Éliante. However, Alceste's determination that the letter be addressed to Oronte incites him to humiliate Célimène and then raise Éliante.

The confrontation between misanthrope and coquette epitomizes comic structure. Alceste's position is reversed from accuser to offender, while both characters perversely present their behavior as models of generosity. The argument again turns on reward for intrinsic worth. Célimène refuses to take seriously Alceste's tragic tone: "O Ciel! de mes transports puis-je être ici le maître?" (IV, iii, 1277). His anger may increase on seeing Célimène, as he declares (1273); but since his last words to Éliante are calm, the audience perceives that he is posturing. Célimène's response draws attention to his gestures—his "soupirs poussés, / Et ces sombres regards" (1279–80); and she responds with a joke to his exaggerated statements that

> . . . toutes les horreurs dont une âme est capable
> À vos déloyautés n'ont rien de comparable;
> Que le sort, les démons et le Ciel en courroux
> N'ont jamais rien produit de si méchant que vous.
>
> (1281–84)

"Voilà certainement des douceurs que j'admire" (1285), she replies. Her attitude and strategy are summed up in pithy dismissals of his rhetorical appeals to fate and justice. The general accusation (1286–1314)—or anathema—does not reduce her to speechlessness. Nothing he threatens elicits a serious response as she consistently deflates his posturing and opens the way to peace.

Her unconvincing explanation that she sent the letter to a woman is a device allowing Alceste a graceful exercise of charity that he should accept. The audience foresees, by the sheer force of repeated structure in the play, that he can win no more now than in act II or with Oronte; consequently, he must either leave Célimène or save face. He cannot yet charitably forgive the fault; accepting the explanation, however, would be better than nothing: it would be an act worthy of an ordinary lover, but not of a particularly generous or charitable one. An extraordinary lover recognizes basic flaws and accepts the defective beloved nevertheless. Alceste is no lover. He refuses the graceful solution, sarcastically commanding Célimène to defend her explanation. She defeats him simply and suddenly by dismissing his opinions as worthless. The argument turns on this notion of value: "Non, je n'en veux rien faire, et, dans cette occurrence / Tout ce que vous croirez m'est de peu d'importance" (1359–60). As in act II, when he questions as proof her verbal assurance that he possesses "le bonheur de savoir que vous êtes aimé"

(II, i, 503), Alceste again fails to take her word on faith; it may be asking too much that he do so, but Alceste himself habitually asks others to recognize his merits on the strength of his word. His refusal to do for his beloved what he demands of everyone prompts Célimène to deny his value—and that provokes a complete deterioration of Alceste's quasi-ethical advantage.

If Célimène will justify the letter, he proposes to feign belief. Alceste is desperate to keep some advantage in the salon over Oronte—which he suspects he does not even have—and he would sacrifice ethical advantage and his distinctive merit, sincerity. But Célimène refuses to accommodate him and debase herself. She employs the elevated vocabulary of sincerity and value to which Alceste is particularly sensitive, and she keeps him dangling with assertions that a man who doubts a woman's word is unworthy of love.

Allez, vous êtes fou dans vos transports jaloux,
Et ne méritez pas l'amour qu'on a pour vous.

(1391–92)

Quoi! de mes sentiments l'obligeante assurance
Contre tous vos soupçons ne prend pas ma défense?

(1397–98)

L'amant qui voit pour lui franchir un tel obstacle
Doit-il impunément douter de cet oracle?

(1405–6)

Allez, de tels soupçons méritent ma colère,
Et vous ne valez pas que l'on vous considère.

(1409–10)

Nevertheless,

Je suis sotte, et veux mal à ma simplicité
De conserver encor pour vous quelque bonté;
Je devrais autre part attacher mon estime
Et vous faire un sujet de plainte légitime.

(1411–14)

Behind her claim of charitable action there lurks the model of a gracious, bountiful power that she imitates perversely, calling attention to the terms of the relationship, asking credit for her generous behavior, and threatening to withdraw favor. She is abusing the model as she has abused Alceste's terminology.

Alceste's exclamation, "Ah! traîtresse" (1415), reinforces this perception, making the rest of his reply surprising: why prolong the relationship if he recognizes her insincerity? He virtually accuses her of malevolence, but claims to follow his destiny. His pseudo-tragic language makes him seem bound to Célimène, as to an evil condition of his existence, without ability or will to overcome it. He also appears to be pushing her character to the limit: "Je veux voir jusqu'au bout quel sera votre coeur, / Et si de me trahir il aura la noirceur" (1419–20). This is not done with impunity before a genuine power, wicked or benevolent.

Alceste cannot accept the idea that Célimène loves him out of the goodness of her heart (on that score he is ironically correct) and not in recognition of his worthiness. He proposes an expression of his love for her which distorts such a relationship of benefactor to undeserving creature and reverses the roles:

Ah! rien n'est comparable à mon amour extrême,
Et, dans l'ardeur qu'il a de se montrer à tous,
Il va jusqu'à former des souhaits contre vous.
Oui, je voudrais qu'aucun ne vous trouvât aimable,
Que vous fussiez réduite en un sort misérable,
Que le Ciel, en naissant, ne vous eût donné rien,
Que vous n'eussiez ni rang, ni naissance, ni bien,
Afin que de mon coeur l'éclatant sacrifice
Vous pût d'un pareil sort réparer l'injustice;
Et que j'eusse la joie et la gloire, en ce jour,
De vous voir tenir tout des mains de mon amour.

(1422–32)

This notion resembles the conceit governing *L'École des femmes*, where Arnolphe would demonstrate, but perversely, a power like the creator's. The misplaced emphasis in these relationships denotes a giving intended to glorify the donor rather than to restore the creature through love to man's original purity, mythologically speaking. Such a gift also contradicts the criterion of merit on which Alceste has insisted. Under stress he reveals a desire to act like the king, without reference to the deserts and defects of those rewarded. He usually demands a reasonable reward for inherent worth instead of arbitrary treatment according to the king's or woman's mysterious grace; now he imagines a situation where he may exercise justice like the model he rejected. His grace, however—his "éclatant sacrifice"—originates in self-love rather than in charity for the person bereft of value. The motive is obligation, not *bonté*—servitude to himself, not liberation from the flaws marring human nature. Alceste will have a chance to act out this fantasy in act V, and Célimène will, justly, refuse it.

Alceste's valet intrudes into this exposition of perversions of generosity with news from the law court, the third place where Alceste does not receive deferential treatment. The act that began with an account of humiliation before the royal marshals ends with a garbled report that Alceste has lost his lawsuit and must flee Paris to avoid arrest. Du Bois's farcical intrusion interrupts Alceste's fantasy of power. The self-styled savior is reduced to an ordinary man in trouble; the situation is again reversed. Du Bois's confusing, broken narrative (unlike Philinte's continuous narration in IV, i) embarrasses Alceste before Célimène because she learns of the court judgment and some undefined imminent danger, and because she witnesses the servant's bumbling manner.

Du Bois also mentions an unidentified man, as anonymous as the one Philinte had greeted to Alceste's annoyance. If acquaintances flatter without committing themselves morally, friends render service when the chips are down. To save Alceste from arrest for something Du Bois cannot explain, this courtier has violated the secrecy of the Royal Law (as Valère does for Orgon in *Le Tartuffe*). A mysterious friend passes once, unseen, through the action, an indicator that Alceste lacks self-sufficiency and that someone does act generously to benefit friends at his peril, without thought of advantage or obligation.

Two other unseen, unnamed figures contribute to Alceste's hatred for mankind and make this anonymous friend stand out sharply: the courtier whom Philinte greeted, and the unsavory Tartuffe-like character who sues Alceste and who, according to a report in v, i, has spread vicious rumors about him. This hypocrite epitomizes the society for Alceste. By contrast, the friend exemplifies the possibility of good works, charitable behavior, and generosity. He risks his safety in divulging a state secret for a friend. Molière places at the end of act IV an example of distinctive ethical behavior that differs from the characteristically selfish action of the play while recalling the noble thoughts of Éliante and Philinte expounded at the beginning of the act. The friend performs a deed (not a gesture) indicating an attitude or philosophy, and as such his act remains unique in the play. The farcical introduction of his warning, however, distracts from its true nature: Alceste is too busy scolding the valet to observe his friend's generosity. Alceste claims distinction for his own merit alone; before Du Bois enters, he imagines he has sufficient worth to endow an impoverished, nullified Célimène with it. He probably would fail to recognize value in anyone else. Since the beginning, he has desired his own distinction: "Je veux qu'on me distingue" (I, i, 63). The joke on him, when act v begins, is that the anonymous friend has provided a model for distinctive behavior indicative of genuine ethical merit, a model for action, not for gesture, and Alceste fails to recognize it, just as he consistently fails to act ethically in his confrontations with Oronte and Célimène.

Although Philinte also demonstrates his worth, his action is less radical and risky than revealing state secrets. He does not abandon Alceste, despite the dangers of associating with a man considered ridiculous. Philinte's attitude toward the corruption Alceste denounces provides another model for distinctive behavior, this one passive and philosophical. In another Lucretian statement (v, i, 1555–69) complementing Éliante's, he proposes an understanding acceptance of flawed human nature and man's monstrosity. His position distinguishes the philosopher from the crowd, even while he remains in contact with it to exercise an ethical program of charity. Philinte tolerates man with his defects, recognizes his own distinction, and knows secret joys (as opposed to the public vanity of courtiers and *salonniers*) in his capacity to judge and pardon his fellows those faults that are theirs not by choice but by the accidents of human nature and the consequences of history. Philinte deems genuine distinction a private ethical attitude; public admiration by flawed men is worthless—an opinion pointing up the paradox in Alceste's desire for recognition from worthless people. Philinte, however, does not condemn the salon or the court from any Olympian distance. He participates unobtrusively in the salon and manages the gestures that keep the society from disintegrating. He greeted the anonymous courtier to avoid the kind of offensive behavior that provokes man, the socialized animal, into uncovering and exercising his defects, the monstrous tendencies that Philinte observes.

In act V his advice applies to the third arena of Alceste's trials, the law court. Alceste could utilize a form provided by justice and appeal the decision (1538–40). There is hope for a reversal as there is for justice at the royal court, which has squelched Oronte's and the hypocrite's scandalous charges, attributing a "livre abominable" to Alceste.

Ce que votre partie ose vous imputer
N'a point eu le crédit de vous faire arrêter;
On voit son faux rapport lui-même se détruire,
Et c'est une action qui pourrait bien lui nuire.

(1527–30)

Something is to be said in favor of a court that discredits irresponsible accusations. But Alceste prefers to lose the case and deny the law court a chance to function justly; he refuses to let an ethical action occur. The demand for public recognition of his merit thus takes another perverse form. He prefers to inveigh against the courts, invoking the privilege he considers to have purchased with the twenty thousand francs in damages he was condemned to pay. Alceste proposes to make his material loss, which would humiliate other men to silence, a pretext for boasting of his virtue and increasing his moral advantage. This is distinctive behavior—distinctive of a fool gesturing wildly instead of seizing the opportunity to restore justice and redeem the system.

Analogously, Alceste fails to act redemptively toward Célimène. Her corruption, laid bare, exceeds the hint of infidelity in the note Arsinoé had given Alceste. By their agreement in act III, Acaste and Clitandre have shown one another letters praising the recipient and disparaging the other rivals. This final series of portraits, read in the subjects' presence, humiliates Célimène who has just been pressed by Oronte and Alceste to commit herself to one and banish the other. Neither wants her any longer. The portraits provoke a mass desertion. The satirical descriptions of Alceste and Oronte, in particular, also allow a surprising insight into the misanthrope's manner of expressing his distinction and provide a succinct summary of the play's concern with merit and civilization.

For all their enmity Oronte and Alceste share a common trait that becomes apparent only now. Célimène identifies them both according to peculiarities of clothing: Alceste as "l'homme aux rubans verts" and Oronte as "l'homme à la veste" (v, iv, paragraphs 4 and 5 in prose between verses 1690 and 1691). For the first time we notice that Alceste affects something odd in his dress. Célimène refers to him within the vestimentary terms of his own satirical model in II, i, where he mocked Clitandre. This late revelation produces a stunning effect. Célimène has thought of Alceste just as he has considered his rivals, in terms of some superficial sign of distinction—a kind of gesture of ornamental clothing with no underlying value. Célimène's reference reduces Alceste to the level of Clitandre, and by his own petard. Green ribbons, fashionable or not, are ornaments intended to draw Alceste attention; they cannot, however, denote his distinctive merit, particularly if color symbolism is considered: green represents folly. (Molière wore green on his costumes: the "médecin malgré lui" wears green and yellow, for example.) By identifying Alceste with ribbons, Célimène makes ornament as important as the moral stance he assumes; she equates the esthetic and superficial with the ethical and essential, and makes the audience suspect that Alceste's program of sincerity is as superficial and borrowed as the ribbons—and equally intended to draw attention to a fictitious worth. The ribbons function as snuff does for Dom Juan's valet, Sganarelle. Ribbons and Oronte's oversized coat are signs of civilization permitting distinction of one person from all others. But they are chosen to denote fortune—or the desire to appear fortunate; they cannot indicate inherent or acquired ethical value.

The vision here is close to that in *King Lear:* ornaments distract from the nakedness of being, from the frailty or nullity that an Alceste and perhaps an Oronte may fear at their very core. The adoption of a moral program and writing of verse may also be signs intended to distract from and patch over the fissures or nullity of our being. The error of such ways, however, is that Alceste and Oronte may have genuine merit, qualities of the *honnête homme*, that Éliante and Philinte recognize; their ambitions for distinction make them abandon virtues for "lendings": a "vaste rhingrave" or a "veste" or green ribbons—or poetasting and inveighing against the times' corruption. Borrowings, characteristics of brilliant civilizations, are signs of decadence when used perversely to disguise or ignore basic truths about man.

The salon is clearly in an advanced state of deterioration when Molière permits Alceste, exposed and humiliated, one final opportunity to redeem Célimène and to reconstruct a relationship with her, honestly this time, without superficial signs to distract from moral values, without the clothing and affectation that encourage a coquette to avoid the values according to which honest judgments and moral commitments are made. Alceste's failure to do so occurs in the context of the selfish, morally blind responses of the other suitors and Arsinoé.

In the last scene the members of her salon enact toward Célimène the scornful gesture of rejection with which Alceste had met them. They also threaten to expose at court the flaw in her character that Acaste and Clitandre acknowledge when they can no longer derive advantage from her. The petits marquis and Oronte dismiss her criticism as malicious. They do not recognize the truth of her characterizations; nor should they, since she intended her sketches not to instruct but to mock her subjects and to produce a false sense of superiority in the recipient of the letter. It is a strange advantage, however, that consists in humiliation of rivals: nothing positive is said about the recipient; he has advantage by comparison with nullity. Like Alceste's denunciations, Célimène's portraits perform no ethical service; they reproduce perversely the just action that reveals truth and prompts self-correction. The purpose of satirical comedy is not humiliation but exposure and conversion; and the authentic satirist who means to chastize and redeem, to humble and elevate, in the manner of Boileau and Pascal, establishes a stance of self-humiliation so that he may expose without appearing arrogant or scornful.

Alceste expects his denunciations to convert no one. He believes human nature incorrigibly corrupt: Dorilas will never stop boring the court; Émilie will always use powder to look younger. He intends to go on record as observing truth without trying to change those whom he scorns. He does say, however, that he expects to cure Célimène of her vices (I, i, 233–34). That would be appropriate for, from Alceste's point of view, a lover may try to recast his beloved in his own image. (Éliante had proposed that a lover does not convert what he loves; his passion allows him to see faults as unique virtues.) Transforming the values of a beloved also involves sacrifice in the lover—a genuinely "éclatant sacrifice": not compromise, but the renunciation of ego and of values that no longer serve (if they ever did) to establish a legitimate, workable relationship. Alceste would rather obligate Célimène to himself and take all the advantage. He is no Cornelian hero like Auguste capable of self-transformation by overcoming deeply rooted moral flaws and generously providing a model of conversion for those he loves to follow.

By infusing Célimène with his values—if indeed he has any— Alceste has the chance to gain, then magnanimously to disregard total advantage over her. The audience may expect such a dramatic turn because in act IV he had already wished desperately, albeit perversely, to pardon Célimène and had fantasized about giving her value. But then, as in act II and earlier in act V, when he and Oronte insisted she choose between them, Alceste had feared rivals, and he had quarreled to obtain definitive proof of his advantage. The plot concerning Célimène, announced in the exposition (I, i), is a series of futile attempts on Alceste's part to make her dismiss her admirers. But in act V the suitors walk out; there is no longer any advantage in being the favorite. The terms are not changed, however, so much as they are finally revealed as they truly apply to Alceste. For he desires Célimène just as his rivals do, as an object he may boast about. Ethically, Alceste belongs to the least common denominator of Acaste and Clitandre, as his clothing connects him to Oronte. Alceste, like Célimène herself, interprets her worth through the specious equation: value equals the number of men she attracts. When the courtiers leave, her appeal vanishes. And that is the time to convert the coquette into an *honnête femme*, to inspire her, by example, to adopt ethical values demonstrated in attitudes and behavior. Alceste's program and character are put to an ultimate test, which he fails through a comic paradox like that regarding his lawsuit.

The suitors gone, he must be rid of Célimène and appear just. She offers herself to him and, simulating generosity, he accepts: he will forget her failings—provided she leave Paris and the court. He must guess, as we do, that exile is intolerable to a twenty-year-old widow. Pardon contigent on an act violating Célimène's being is neither just behavior nor genuine, free pardon; it allows Alceste to humiliate Célimène, to expose her worthlessness should she refuse his conditions. His dismissal, as he turns from her, is the final example of his characteristic gesture; but here it definitively denotes his misunderstanding of the dynamics governing the recognition of values, or their absence, and the creation *ex nihilo* of workable ethical values. Alceste fails to convert a woman and to furnish a model for a just society in her transformation.

An additional circumstance magnifies the force of his humiliating gesture and its boomeranging effect upon Alceste. The contrite Célimène virtually begs Alceste to rescue her from her errors and from the nullity to which the courtiers' denunciation will diminish her. We recognize her desperation and are briefly satisfied as she faces her judge and as Alceste seems to respond favorably. But

Molière frustrates any anticipation of a "happy" or heroic resolution. Alceste only seems to offer pardon. He does not embrace Célimène, for that act now is useless to indicate privilege. An embrace, however, would denote more than advantage: it would signify love. Alceste casts her aside and refuses to raise her from humiliation. He misses the chance to transform the empty gesture of embracing into the kiss of peace and charity in the act to which the play's esthetic design leads. Alceste had considered embracing a perverse means of gaining advantage and creating obligation. Now he has finally the rare opportunity to imitate properly the bountiful powers who forgive and redeem imperfect and fallible human beings. Alceste hates mankind for its corruption; but he is most perverse when he ignores the possibility of rescuing one sinner from her fallen state and of acquiring the heroic, noble qualities we as spectators desire in ourselves as well as in him. Alceste might, by his example, show us the way to overcome our own human limitations. Would we—could we—expose ourselves to the possibility of ridicule by risking a saving, graceful action on a desperate person who has previously shown no sign of moral sensitivity?

The ambiguity of the audience's response to Alceste's abandoning Célimène and fleeing Paris is central to the moral program underlying French classical thought as exemplified not only in Molière's comedies but in the heroic tragedies of Corneille, La Fontaine's *Fables*, and Pascal's *Pensées*. We have grounds both to sympathize with Alceste and to speculate on the results of some unexpected radical act. The ethical pattern in the play's world, as misunderstood by the characters, has proved bankrupt. Perhaps a break with ordinary behavior—an act based on a more accurate idea of the loving relationships between the sources of authority and the men who desire power—might create another, more human order.

The High Renaissance of the seventeenth century in France sought to rescue man from old and crippling interpretations of Christian mythologies and to place him within a new ideology based on humanist precedents. These harked back to Roman philosophical traditions of Stoicism and Epicureanism. The learned free thought of the period—the *libertinage érudit*—attempted to construct an ethic severed from the Christian dogma that makes man a miserable doomed creature instead of an active part of creation or Nature, responsible for his own just behavior without reference to a Fall or supernatural redemption. Alceste is given and misses the opportunity to found such an ethic in a pardon that duplicates the generosity of the French Renaissance prince—in the manner of Rabelais's rulers—and the God for whose aid and forgiveness the true Christian humanist hopes.

The audience, however, is also unprepared to bridge the gulf between abandoning our humiliated Célimènes and giving them rebirth by conversion to genuine values. We cannot condemn Alceste without implicating ourselves in his guilt; and if we find him faultless, we must be missing something too. The strategy resembles La Fontaine's; he makes us laugh with the final line in the first fable: "Eh bien, dansez maintenant," jokes the ant to the grasshopper starving to death. If this realization does not stop our laughter, we are as heartless as the industrious–miserly, virtuous–vicious neighbor. We must realize what the stakes are for ourselves, identifying as we do with the ant. We resist identifying with the desperate grasshopper, although most of us need sustenance that must be borrowed. How many readers pity the grasshoppers of life? Who can act spontaneously in the elevated manner of Corneille's heroic figures, Auguste, César, Nicomède—all played by Molière, incidentally—or can imitate their extraordinary ethical heroism in the manner of the converted Cinna and Attale?

The final act in Corneille's most effective tragedies stuns us because it occurs unexpected by characters and audience, and because it lies beyond our range of action. Heroism occurs as extraordinary action that a spectator admires—wonders at—because it strikes him as impossible for himself. If Chimène refuses to marry Rodrigue, that is heroic: extraordinary, in the sense that we cannot imagine her—or ourselves—not capitulating to love and desire, Rodrigue's devotion, the king's command. Corneille's dramaturgy leads to this point: the audience's reaction to accumulated circumstances and to knowledge that the characters lack differs from the protagonist's solution. We foresee only a pedestrian response: cut the knot or give in. The hero's astonishing action renews our sense of human values and worth: not what I am capable of as an individual, but what man can do in the face of adversity, accident, fate. Cornelian tragedy concerns such values: a surprising radical break with expected, ordinary behavior and attitudes; concomitant renunciation of established but futile ways and human ego; consequent gain of extraordinary merit, ranging from simple recognition of the hero's worth, as with Chimène and Horace, all the way to the quasi divinization of Auguste and César.

Alceste, like Dom Juan, styles himself a hero in the Cornelian mold who deliberately challenges society's values. But if he behaves shockingly at first, finally he neither amazes nor inspires conversion to other values. No Cornelian miracle takes place. The audience is nevertheless permitted to respond in a manner inseparable from tragic experience, although not with the admiration typical of the Cornelian mode. We have the opportunity to extend compassion to Alceste after he fails to pardon Célimène, to do for him what he did not accomplish for her, and, in the process, to experience compassion for ourselves who also could not have behaved heroically. Comedy's function is not to condemn miser, social climber, *grand seigneur méchant homme*, or even the religious hypocrite, but to make us reconsider the bases of our values by projecting versions of the basic relationships that structure our lives. Comedy makes us acknowledge our weaknesses: with power and freedom from condemnation and punishment, we too would participate in perverse imitations of those essential relationships. Compassion and forgiveness, or at the very least an understanding of our ordinary incapacity for ethical action, are extended by the king in *Tartuffe* (who shows the way to a vengeful Orgon), by Anselme in *L'Avare*, by Arnolphe's old friends in *L'École des femmes*, by the princess in *Dom Garcie de Navarre;* only in *Dom Juan* is God's compassion frustrated, and he is compelled to destroy

the perverter of human and divine values. In *Le Misanthrope* no exterior authority intervenes to teach compassion. The exemplar of
generosity is the friend who pursues Alceste with love and wisdom
from the beginning. True to his name, Philinte shows us the way.
His behavior, while less heroic than an Auguste's, is still extraordinary within the play's context of perversions of friendship. Philinte
imitates the bountiful power's self-sacrifice to create a new valid
order among men that lies within the range of the audience's powers.

After Alceste's quasi-noble posturings in releasing Éliante and
declaring his intention to forsake corrupt mankind, and his failure
to establish his value in the only authentic way–ethical behavior
following the model of king's or God's free pardon—Philinte ends
the play as a friend still committed to serving him. Instead of celebrating Philinte's engagement to Éliante, in observation of the
marriage that normally concludes comedy, Molière terminates the
play with a statement of this friend's loyalty, a genuine advantage
about which Philinte never boasts: "Allons, madame, allons em-
ployer toute chose / Pour rompre le dessein que son coeur se propose"
(1807–8). Philinte neither wonders, as we may, whether Alceste's
heart is "creux et plein d'ordure," nor asks whether he has belied
his name's dual classical associations with Alcides–Hercules and
Alcestis, the one celebrated for trials of physical strength, the other
for love so strong she would sacrifice life itself for her husband in
a supreme ethical test. Alcides, the devoted friend of Alcestis' husband, redeems her. He does not question the worth of a husband
who lets his wife die for him; in true friendship he overlooks the
failing and establishes a basis for the free, human relationship un-
fettered by obligation, real or contrived, that is imitated in *Le Misanthrope* in various perverse forms—except by Philinte and Éliante.
They exemplify the noble values and the human dignity to which
Alceste's name alludes and which provide a background against
which Molière's comic theater—and comedy itself—might be better
understood.

·4·

JUSTICE FOR
GEORGE DANDIN

George Dandin might be considered Molière's cynical comedy: because appearances conspire to make its protagonist, who is morally right, look morally wrong, he finally chooses suicide to escape a desperate situation. That interpretation, however, ignores the perspective implicit in the play's structure which allows him the opportunity to resolve his dilemma. Since he will not take a chance and run the risk of exposure once again to ridicule, he loses definitively any possibility of happiness. The peasant misallied to a provincial noblewoman might be a spiritual relative not so far removed of Alceste's. Each adopts the posture of the just man wronged who seeks justice, and each fails to establish valid, workable ethical relationships with the woman he has chosen, who pleads desperately for pardon. The ultimate laugh is on George Dandin even in his despair, because he denies his wife the spirit of justice, pardon, while he is refused the letter of justice that he demands. Like Alceste, he epitomizes the unjust man who asks justice of others. *George Dandin* is a reworking in farcical mode of the obsession dominating the high comedy of *Le Misanthrope*.

A model of action recurs according to a regular rhythm. George Dandin, disenchanted with his marital situation, gathers evidence that he confidently presents to his in-laws, expecting them to acknowledge their daughter's guilt; his despair deepens as appearances turn against him and he is condemned, more intensely in each succeeding act. The play takes the form of a series of trials, with Dandin as plaintiff, Angélique as defendant, and the Sotenvilles as judges. Dandin summons his in-laws to confront them with prima facie evidence: ". . . j'ai en main de quoi vous faire voir comme elle m'accommode et, Dieu merci! mon déshonneur est si clair maintenant, que vous n'en pourrez plus douter" (II, vii). He refuses to understand that these judges cannot afford simple justice. They do not take his word against their daughter's and a nobleman's because their finances are at stake. In frustration—"J'enrage d'avoir tort lorsque j'ai raison"—he apologizes. By the time the model has been repeated in act III, it seems that the comic rhythm could continue indefinitely, except that after Dandin refuses to risk pardoning Angélique, our interest in him can no longer be sustained: even Dandin must admit that he has failed irremediably.

Reconciliation is impossible once Dandin rejects a basis for it in an ethic supplanting the defective values to which he had assented and which militate against him. The ideology remaining at the end is the Sotenvilles' mythology of their nobility: delusions of grandeur and ancestral traditions that do not correspond to their own actions. Dandin has sought to acquire aristocratic value in the wrong place and by illegitimate means; at the end he perceives his in-laws' valueless nature. The provincial Sot-en-villes do not represent the genuine aristocracy; their name indicates the mockery awaiting them in Versailles and Paris. They point to a distinction between spurious— or outworn—and genuine sources of nobility and values.

Before the civil wars of the mid-seventeenth century, the Fronde, the aristocracy could proudly honor ancestral values, actively renewing the idea of genealogically claimed nobility based on feudal power and service to the crown. Cornelian *devoir* and *générosité* reflect the nobility's strong ethical attitudes and codes of behavior based on them. But the Cornelian terms become pretextual catchwords whose significance must be rethought, even renewed, in the course of a play by some unexpected action that inspires wonder and the desire to emulate it. It is a question of embracing new ethical attitudes as a basis for *générosité*, instead of claiming nobility through adherence to the traditional values and celebrated deeds of an ancient class or clan—the *genus* from which *générosité* etymologically derives. The Fronde showed the political dangers inherent in a nobility that could exercise its sense of traditional values and prerogatives, and the Sun King set out to reduce the aristocracy entirely to his service. For a La Rochefoucauld, however, deprived of the possibility of heroic action (along with an entire class of nobles who lost in the Fronde), true nobility becomes a question of ethical attitude, not one of independent deed. The *Maximes* are a distillation of his ethics, in which the idea of nobility shifts from the category of physical activity to an enduring expression of intellect and moral attitude. Given a nobility as philosophically inclined as La Rochefoucauld's, this genealogy of noble values might have replaced the older one celebrating ancestral deeds; it did not, however, take root in late seventeenth-century France, for the ethics of the aristocracy through the end of the ancien régime remained distinct from the humanistic values Molière also envisages as a viable alternative.

Such a distinction is indicated in act III, scene vi, by, of all people, Angélique. Dandin's proofs of her infidelity have grown increasingly strong—the comic rhythm intensifies the action—while his despair and frustration have grown apace. Angélique, compromised after her nocturnal rendezvous, fears she cannot explain to her parents' satisfaction why she is locked out. She appeals to Dandin, confesses guilt, pleads for mercy. Dandin acquires the additional privileged role of judge as, also for this one time, Angélique agrees to honor his authority. That power had earlier been based on a legal contract in which she had participated under duress. Now she offers to submit to an authority established on other grounds. This scene raises the possibility of conversion to moral values through the ex- ample of behavior liberated from all past claims, legitimate or not. In a paradigm of just action, forgiveness and the renunciation of self-interest would permit redemption of the person pardoned and the consequent pursuit of a happy, ethical life. Is Angélique's pro- posal credible?

Dandin characterizes his wife as wicked; the audience perceives Angélique as a victim of parents who exchanged her for Dandin's wealth to maintain dilapidated nobility. Even Dandin admits this: "L'alliance qu'ils font est petite avec nos personnes: c'est notre bien seul qu'ils épousent" (I, i). He reminds the Sotenvilles that "sans moi vos affaires, avec votre permission, étaient fort délabrées, et mon argent a servi à reboucher d'assez bons trous" (I, iv). Angélique tells Dandin that she has no illusions on that score, either (II, ii). Whether the audience approves or condemns her flirtation with Clitandre, it enjoys her bold manipulations of situation and language to encourage the suitor (I, vi, and II, viii) and to combat confinement. Sympathy for a young woman abused and defending herself reinforces the pleasure of traditional farce in Angélique's double entendres, her beating of Dandin while pretending to hit her suitor (II, vii), and Dandin's deserved cuckoldry. An unjust man deserves heartless treatment, which should not necessarily be imputed to a cruel nature. Besides, her parents' values have set the example of unethical behavior. They refuse in acts I and II to acknowledge her misdeeds in order to avoid returning Dandin's money should the couple separate. She must fear their anger once, unmarriageable, she returns home. Facing that possibility, no better than marriage to a peasant, Angélique pleads for different values to end her parents' tyranny and to inaugurate respect and perhaps even love between herself and Dandin.

The vocabulary of nobility suddenly springing from Angélique indicates that she recognizes other values besides those corrupting her. She seems ready for a secular version of grace. She may be insincere; in that case she debases ethical language to empty rhetoric. But to impute fraudulent motives to her is to shift the focus and miss the point of Dandin's insensitivity to noble values and his incapacity to see beyond immediate self-interest. We perceive a joke on the man who cannot recognize that renunciation of advantage may create relationships satisfying the joint interests of husband and wife as egoism yields to a generosity inspiring respect and admiration. Physical force and contractual obligation are replaced by moral dominion, which is different from domination since people transformed by generous action behave according to noble values that constitute a newly created morality. Everyone who imitates the idea of nobility participates in ethical dominion; there are neither superiors nor slaves.

Dandin, by nature and practice unjust and ungenerous, expects justice finally to deal fairly according to regulation. He will not give up the legal advantage of evidence that Angélique's confession provides; he does not suspect that her vocabulary of grace and pardon, accompanied by contrite gestures, affords him another order of advantage which, should he renounce it, might establish the condition of a happy marriage and a nobility independent of the Sotenvilles' false values. He refuses to take a risk in response to the despair that Angélique expresses repeatedly in this scene:

> Je confesse que j'ai tort, et que vous avez sujet de vous plaindre. Mais je vous demande par grâce de ne m'exposer point maintenant à la mauvaise humeur de mes parents . . .

> De grâce, laissez-moi vous dire. Je vous demande un moment d'audience.

> Votre ressentiment est juste. . . . Ce sont des actions que vous devez pardonner à mon âge . . .

> Je ne veux point m'excuser par là d'être coupable envers vous, et je vous prie seulement d'oublier une offense dont je vous demande pardon de tout mon coeur, et de m'épargner en cette rencontre le déplaisir que me pourraient causer les reproches fâcheux de mon père et de ma mère. Si vous m'accordez généreusement la grâce que je vous demande, ce procédé obligeant, cette bonté que vous me ferez voir, me gagnera entièrement. Elle touchera tout à fait mon coeur, et y fera naître pour vous ce que tout le pouvoir de mes parents et les liens du mariage n'avaient pu y jeter. En un mot, elle sera cause que je renoncerai à toutes les galanteries, et n'aurai de l'attachement que pour vous. Oui, je vous donne ma parole que vous m'allez voir désormais la meilleure femme du monde, et que je vous témoignerai tant d'amitié, tant d'amitié, que vous en serez satisfait.

Acknowledging the conventional but futile justice of Dandin's anger, Angélique asks him to master his wrath. Like Livie in *Cinna*, she opens up previously unsuspected moral perspectives: pardon, moral example, conversion. An authentic bond between the pardoner and the person redeemed would replace the fictitious gap in natures on which the Sotenvilles harp. The peasant whom market exchange did not ennoble is invited to create a true aristocracy based on an ethical act reflecting generosity of spirit—not genealogy, memories, or ancestral claims like the military events of dubious value cited by Monsieur de Sotenville (I, vi).

Dandin, however, prefers the certainty that Angélique's parents will condemn her and release him from the marriage. He misses the lesson indicated by the comic rhythm of the earlier acts, that the situation will again be reversed if he presses his case—and his luck. By failing to wager on the side of the angels, so to speak, Dandin commits the fatal error that leads to his undoing, when he might have broken the old vicious pattern to inaugurate a new paradigm of behavior. The comic rhythm reasserts itself: Angélique, denied pardon, has no choice but to revert to character and dupe him. He gets his just deserts: he has exercised the reverse of the "procédé obligeant" called for; as usual, in Sotenville's earlier words, "votre procédé met tout le monde contre vous" (I, iv). "Tout le monde" now includes the audience. We would not extend sympathy even if Dandin committed suicide as threatened; his last monologue provokes laughter because, even while acknowledging his error in marrying a "méchante femme" Dandin has refused the opportunity to convert her and make possible his own happiness and hers.

> Ah! je le quitte maintenant, et je n'y vois plus de remède; lorsqu'on a, comme moi, épousé une méchante femme, le meilleur parti qu'on puisse prendre, c'est de s'aller jeter dans l'eau la tête la première. (III, viii)

Molière again violates the convention which excludes death from comedy. The version presented at court was part of a ballet whose concluding celebration of love and Bacchus, to which Dandin was forcibly led, sweetened the ending. Lully's pastoral for the king was designed to please, not to disturb. At the Paris performances which omitted the dances, the audience was left with the ethical problem and with the impression that Dandin still presented himself as an example for a whole class of men. He is no longer a "leçon bien parlante" only for social-climbing peasants as he announces at the beginning. He still blames other people for his troubles. Early in the play he attributes them to the nobility, as though it had forced him into marriage: the nobles "nous font, nous autres, entrer dans leur famille" (I, i). He makes his case seem to represent a general phenomenon of widespread intermarriage amongst the social orders. He tries to project the image of a virtuous man, deceived, who acknowledges his folly—"Vous avez fait une sottise"—and who is determined to expose his wife's wickedness as an example and as grounds for divorce, making public his disgrace and forcing his in-laws to condemn their daughter's behavior.

Now, were Dandin indeed a fair man, he would be entitled to justice in the ideal world of comedy, where justice, tempered with merciful understanding of human defects, is extended finally even to the unjust, as in, for example, *Dom Juan, Measure for Measure, The Tempest, Lysistrata.* But Dandin's injustice underlies all his deeds: his loveless, unequal marriage violates the traditional order; he purchased a wife to obtain a spurious nobility. Angélique explains (II, ii) that she never consented to a marriage that is a legalized rape. We also find disturbing a man who shouts his dishonor from the rooftops. No honorable man would utter the curtain line ending the second act: "Ô Ciel, seconde mes desseins, et m'accorde la grâce de faire voir aux gens que l'on me déshonore." By "gens" he means his in-laws; but his posing as an example makes "people" more inclusive. He must appeal to the audience, much as Harpagon begs for the return of his strongbox. We ridicule the pleas for sympathy because we agree with George Dandin's own words: "Vous l'avez voulu, vous l'avez voulu, George Dandin, vous l'avez voulu, cela vous sied fort bien, et vous voilà ajusté comme il faut; vous avez justement ce que vous méritez" (II, vii). We witness Dandin's violent gestures of self-punishment: he strikes his forehead as he repeats the phrase "vous l'avez voulu" (put in the formal plural form, incidentally: one wonders why); and we are pleased by the sarcastic pun on "ajusté" and "justement"—fixed and justly. The audience recognizes that

Sotenville unjustly condemns Dandin to apologize to Clitandre, who had indeed approached Angélique; but Dandin's choice of such a judge—and such a father-in-law—displays his own lack of equitable values. He has fixed himself but good.

Although he has properly analyzed the Sotenvilles' motives in contracting marriage with him, Dandin remains naïve about their cynicism. Otherwise he could not continually expect them to believe his proofs of Angélique's infidelity. They care nothing for evidence or points of law except those dictating proper forms of address: not "ma belle-mère" and "Monsieur de Sotenville" but "Madame" and "Monsieur"—"tout court" (I, iv). They cannot afford a separation. Dandin does not perceive the cynicism which accepts as normal the exercise of justice exclusively according to the judge's self-interest. Cynics expect no justice. Dandin does: failing to learn from experience, he persists in expecting his in-laws to find Angélique guilty as charged. (The comic rhythm may also make us cynical about the situation, for we do understand that Dandin will not be treated justly.) But for all his naïveté Dandin is cynical in taking a wife to gain a title, without regard for her will or value as a person, and expecting her to cooperate. It is appropriate and comically just that the Sotenvilles judge cynically, according to their interests and without respect for Dandin's value as a person, and that they cynically refuse, in feigned naïveté, to believe that their daughter could dishonor their glorious name.

Dandin's cynicism is one mark of his injustice; attributing his distress to the nobility is another. Yet this unjust man naïvely demands justice of judges whose cynicism he observes in his first monologue. His suicide indicates recognition that they will not be persuaded. But he still refuses to admit his own fault: he shifts the blame to his "méchante femme." In effect, how wicked or cynical is Angélique?

If cynicism includes the attitude that justice deserved never occurs, then Angélique is not cynical. (The play itself in those terms is anything but cynical in outlook: Dandin gets exactly what he deserves on the basis of his actions and through them.) She forthrightly warns her husband that she will treat him as he merits; "pour votre punition," she will "jouir, s'il vous plaît, de quelque nombre de beaux jours que m'offre la jeunesse, prendre les douces libertés que l'âge me permet, voir un peu le beau monde, et goûter le plaisir de m'ouïr dire des douceurs" (II, ii). She has a point. She expresses values which, while not exactly ethical for a wife, belong to a young woman who only normally wants to enjoy youth and beauty. She resembles the emotionally aroused Agnès; the name *Angèle*, of which *Angélique* is a variant, is practically an anagram of the heroine's name in *L'École des femmes*. Her name may be ironic to Dandin but not to anyone who perceives in it possibilities for experiences appropriate to an adolescent growing aware of her beauty. She does, however, utilize her parents' cynicism in the three judgment scenes, confident that they can ill afford to doubt her word. She is no model wife; nor does she pretend to be one when confronting Dandin in act II: he deserves none. We do not have to abandon conventional morality to sympathize with her as she tells Dandin off. Her frankness may extend to act III when she pleads for mercy and promises repentance and conversion. This appeal to the generosity of a potentially just man points to a rupture of the comic rhythm, to a breaking of the vicious circle of cynicism and naïveté, and toward the vision of Cornelian heroic tragedy exemplified by *Cinna* (and by Shakespearean comedy). But, as in *Le Misanthrope*, the opportunity passes. Dandin continues to pursue his perverse imitation of just relationships among men, ignoring the superior order of which Molière hints through Angélique's appeal. Because George Dandin redeems neither wife nor self, he is the object of laughter in this bleak comedy which publicly ridicules a man who refuses to risk possible humiliation after pardoning his wife. He prefers the sure thing; he has no faith in his wife's nature. Is that because he has just as little confidence in his own? And is he alone?

Of the laughing spectators in the theater, who would not act like Alceste or George Dandin? Is anyone without cynicism or naïveté? Does anyone expect justice according to deserts or mercy despite unworthiness? Who does take ethical risks, exposing himself to humiliation? Few Don Quixotes stand up in our midst. There is a difference, however, between ourselves and the Dandin we ridicule: we do not present ourselves as exemplars of justice. We may think privately of ourselves as just men, but we do not make the claim in public: we prefer not to discuss our justice or injustice. Dandin invites mockery as the man who claims to be just, who refuses risk, and, preferring his wife's certain condemnation, is himself condemned and sentenced to live eternally with her. We may question the sincerity of Angélique's appeal and assume that she is cynically engaging in another ruse to take advantage of her husband's stupidity. The comic rhythm supports these prejudices and expectations induced by traditions of farce, the Boccaccian tale, the *fabliaux*. But the tale by Boccaccio that Molière may have used as the basis for the play[1] contains in its corresponding episode no ethical solution proposed by the unfaithful wife; nor is such a suggestion likely in subsequent variants of the traditional comic tale of the cuckold familiar to Molière's audience, which would be sensitive to any significant transformation Molière introduced. His *mari confondu* remains true to the line of cuckolds revitalized in La Fontaine's *Contes*. Angélique, on the other hand, desires to leave the ranks of victimized and unfaithful wives; and, from our safe vantage point in the theater, we can risk allowing her one chance, for we see the enormous potential profit: there is nothing to lose and everything to gain. In our own life, however, do we follow through? The matter of her sincerity remains irrelevant, while the important question raised as we laugh at Dandin is: "Are *we* serious?" Comic satire is pointless—it cannot correct our mores—unless it brings into the open our unspoken attitudes and makes us consider seriously our just and unjust behavior. The esthetic experience of comedy produces the ethical experience of self-scrutiny and self-transformation.

Dandin's refusal to bet on his wife's sincerity leaves her no choice

---

1. Antoine Adam cites the tale in the *Decameron*, book 7, ch. 4, but he doubts that Molière knew or used it directly. *Histoire de la littérature française au dix-septième siècle*, vol. 3 (Paris: Domat, 1952), p. 368.

but to deal with him as he now clearly deserves since he has failed to grasp her exposition of an ideology of ethical values. The comic rhythm leads to a point where an essential relationship may or may not be properly imitated, where justice may or may not spring into existence. If we worry over Angélique's sincerity—and her previous actions do give us pause—then like Dandin we miss a chance to act freely and extend grace to a flawed person; we become trapped in our habits and conventions—in our own comic rhythm—and we never discover our nobility. Angélique's "sincerity" tests us along with Dandin. We do not wish to appear foolish should she (or the person begging us) prove unfaithful to a promise. But the merit of pardon is the pardoner's. The freedom of will and ethical value that he demonstrates—*that he creates in imitation of God's*—will shield him from ridicule. But Dandin is willful without being master of self or universe: his are the desires of a petty, conventional, vindictive morality.

His insistence is associated with getting the opposite of what he bargains for: "Vous l'avez voulu, vous l'avez voulu, George Dandin, vous l'avez voulu," his typical phrase, denotes stubbornness and violence. The protagonist of this farce beats himself, literally. Those blows to the forehead epitomize the violence of his justice. He cannot satisfy his urge to beat his wife, lest she leave him before he obtains a full refund on the purchase price: ". . . l'on vous accommode de toutes pièces, sans que vous puissiez vous venger, et la gentilhom-merie vous tient les bras liés. . . . Si c'était une paysanne, vous auriez maintenant toutes vos coudées franches à vous en faire la justice à bons coups de bâton" (I, iii). Instead, he beats himself, still blaming the nobility for the error of his willfulness. This perverse form of justice—expressed in his analysis of guilt and the violence of his punishment—persists to the end when he announces his in-tention to jump headfirst into a well. Dandin remains a model of the unjust man; but finally he is the unjust man who, having declined to risk an action of another, unaccustomed order—charity—con-demns himself to death, unjustly. His reasoning is wrong: the fault is his. And he remains a consistently ignoble peasant. There are no risks in his death; suicide is part of his comic rhythm. The last act is an imitation of the converse of Montaigne's observation—in the essay "Divers Evenemens de mesme conseil" (book 1, ch. 24) which is the source for *Cinna*—that Pascal repeats: "Rien de noble ne se faict sans hazard."

·5·

VALUES IN
LE BOURGEOIS GENTILHOMME

The announcement of Dorimène's entrance in act III of *Le Bourgeois gentilhomme* provokes a surprising movement of alarm in Monsieur Jourdain. He suddenly lacks the self-confidence exhibited in each previous encounter with teachers, wife, servant, and the aristocrat Dorante. Since the play began, he had been anticipating Dorimène's arrival: the episodes of acts I and II constitute a plot only because Jourdain has engaged instructors, artists, and artisans to help him court her. Molière converts an ingenious character sketch into a drama by using Dorimène's visit as the central event of the plot. It is the reason for Jourdain's special pains on this particular day regarding his own appearance; it is also a cause for anxiety as he anticipates a critical test of his identity.

Dorimène's impending visit is brought to the fore at every turn. The scene with the dancing master leads to Jourdain's request for a "révérence pour saluer une marquise . . . une marquise qui s'appelle Dorimène" (II, i); the music and ballets in preparation during act I are intended to entertain Dorimène, as is the "ballet des nations" that closes the play; and the scene with the maître de philosophie (II, iv) culminates in Jourdain's unwitting display of virtuosity as a writer of prose in his billet-doux to Dorimène. Why he had preferred lessons in "l'orthographe" to logic, moral philosophy,

This chapter appeared in somewhat different form in *L'Esprit Créateur* (1975), 15:105–18. Reprinted by permission.

and physics becomes clear in retrospect at the end of the scene: he would like to know how to spell his love letters. He had also wanted to learn about the "almanach, pour savoir quand il y a de la lune et quand il n'y en a point": courtship and moonlight go hand in hand.

Molière joins plot to theme, courtship to Jourdain's attempt to acquire aristocratic values through material means. All the while, acts I and II have the appearance of a series of sketches between Jourdain and his serving, mocking, serious, ironic artists and artisans. The construction of these scenes, however, produces a sense of Dorimène's significance which imposes on the incidents a coherent pattern in support of the main theme. Esthetics (the construction of plot and arrangement of juxtaposed and congruent actions) join inseparably to ethics (theme and moral structure). Jourdain's ideas of Dorimène link esthetics and ethics in acts I and II. So, when her arrival is at hand, the preceding context has conditioned the audience to take special notice of Jourdain's panic.

The announcement of her entrance occurs in III, xiv, a scene consisting of two short speeches by Jourdain and one by a lackey who does not name Dorimène; she is simply "une dame" accompanied by Dorante, who is familiar enough to Jourdain's household to be called "Monsieur le Comte": "Monsieur, voici Monsieur le Comte, et une dame qu'il mène par la main." Given the preparations for Dorimène's entertainment with which Molière had loaded the play, Jourdain's reaction is puzzling: "Hé mon Dieu! j'ai quelques ordres à donner. Dis-leur que je vais venir ici tout à l'heure." Has he developed a case of the jitters, fearing that this noblewoman will recognize him for what he really is, and in his lackey's presence to boot? Or is he a lover suddenly flustered by his lady's presence, at a loss for words, trying to compose himself? He may of course simply want to make a spectacular entrance with the bow he had practiced with the dancing master. That is how he does in fact enter in III, xvi.

Even if a spectator does not try to explain Jourdain's swift departure, he must wonder why Molière bothered bringing Jourdain back to the stage for such a short appearance. The structural detail—

the brief return of the major character whom we expect to remain and dominate the action—makes us uneasy. Audiences react in terms of character; only after a performance do they recall details and ponder their thematic significance. But the dramatist may often use unexpected or aberrant behavior for thematic purposes that will later mesh with the play's overall design and meaning. In this instance, how may we explain the structural function of Jourdain's sudden appearance and disappearance just before Dorimène's long-anticipated entrance?

Molière had to clear the stage so that Dorante and Dorimène could enter an empty room. The audience must learn about Dorante's own courtship of Dorimène, using Jourdain's entertainment and diamond—which makes her Dorante's dupe as well. Both marquise and bourgeois are involved in relationships of exchange and obligation under false pretenses. Molière could have introduced the couple effectively after the scene at III, xiii, between Cléonte and Covielle, which serves to announce the Turkish ceremony. Covielle could have warned Cléonte that Dorante and Dorimène, rather than Jourdain, were approaching. Jourdain's return after an interval of absence, however, renews the context for Dorimène's entrance at the comedy's thematic and physical center. Molière's manipulation of Jourdain's entrance and flight constitutes an esthetic control that heightens the audience's awareness of the ethical questions at issue.

Jourdain's remarks during his brief reappearance—the play's only monologue—reveal why he is attracted to the aristocracy:

> Que diable est-ce là! ils n'ont rien que les grands seigneurs à me reprocher; et moi, je ne vois rien de si beau que de hanter les grands seigneurs: il n'y a qu'honneur et civilité avec eux, et je voudrais qu'il m'eût coûté deux doigts de la main et être né comte ou marquis.

To Jourdain, aristocracy means *rien de si beau . . . honneur . . . civilité*: esthetic values, ethical values, pleasant gestures translating beautiful sentiments and thought, all the consequence of birth and breeding—and all the contrary of what he experiences in his own household. Up to this point act III, in which members of Jourdain's family first appear, has consisted of nothing but dissension. If for two acts Molière has permitted Jourdain to import beauty into his home, he finally shows the real unpleasantness of the bourgeois domestic situation.

Act III begins with a quarrel between Jourdain and Nicole, continues in an argument between Jourdain and his wife, and leads to the double *dépit amoureux* between Cléonte and Lucile, Covielle and Nicole. When the lovers' quarrel is settled, another disagreement follows Jourdain's rejection of Cléonte's suit. The sequence that began with Nicole—a servant—literally laughing in Jourdain's face ends as Cléonte tells Jourdain that he would rather be a real bourgeois than a bogus nobleman. Into this atmosphere, so strikingly different from Jourdain's vision of beauty, honor, and civility, Dorimène makes her entrance. She is not to be seen, then, simply as the aristocrat Jourdain would woo and conquer, but as the authentic "dame noble" announced by the lackey, the ideal incarnation of the values that are absent in Jourdain's unbeautiful, uncivil, unpleasant household, where servant, wife, daughter, and suitor all seem determined to undermine his authority, less for sanity's sake than for convenience and appearances. Jourdain's teachers mess up the house, objects Nicole, while his wife is worried mostly that the neighbors will observe his madness. Jourdain's experience in act III and his speech in scene xiv define a context where Dorimène appears as the opposite of a distasteful mode of life.

This brief scene, III, xiv, serves esthetically, then, to alert the audience to the ethical problem of value, real or imagined, that Dorimène crystallizes at the play's center. The line of plot has led to a moment where the principal questions are these: Does Jourdain's vision of aristocratic values correspond to any reality? And, if so, does Dorimène incarnate them, or does she, like Dorante, present a specious example of aristocratic behavior?

The audience must wonder why Jourdain succinctly identifies aristocracy with beauty, honor, and civility, rather than with privilege and admiration, although his subsequent exaggeration about giving up two fingers tempers the effect of that equation. His comment makes Jourdain seem ridiculous, but it does not invalidate his perception of the esthetic and ethical values he imputes to aristocrats and would like to find in himself. The audience, however, would like to know just how accurately Jourdain has observed aristocratic behavior, since Dorante, the only nobleman in the play thus far, treats him in the same way that Dom Juan handles Monsieur Dimanche, keeping him off with gestures of civility without the least shred of ethical content. Dorante observes the manners of beauty, honor, and civility, but the audience, like Madame Jourdain, perceives this formal imitation as abuse: she openly mocks him, understanding that he cannot deliver the best seats at a court spectacle (III, v). Lacking the honesty expected of an aristocrat-*honnête homme*, Dorante is a problematic figure. But real values, existing and observable among aristocrats, are less in question here than those that Jourdain attributes to nobles whom he does not know directly. Since in his naïve and hopeful way of thinking, aristocracy is inseparable from the loftiest values, Jourdain extrapolates ethical content from visible forms and gestures to define aristocracy. With Dorimène's entrance and her subsequent speeches and behavior, the reality of the values that Jourdain associates with aristocracy is pointedly tested.

Dorimène's first speeches deal essentially with her embarrassment at Dorante's courtship, which she sees as a process of obligation meant to force her into marriage. She regrets her own complacency and her inadequate resistance to the influence of his presents and magnificent gestures. She is initially concerned over coming to a strange house against her will, as if something shameful about Dorante's courtship were to be hidden: "Je ne sais pas, Dorante, je fais encore ici une étrange démarche, de me laisser amener par vous dans une maison où je ne connais personne." More serious is her fear that Dorante's attentions, typified by the entertainment arranged in Jourdain's *hôtel particulier*, increase her obligation to her suitor:

Mais vous ne dites pas que je m'engage insensiblement, chaque jour, à recevoir de trop grands témoignages de votre passion? J'ai beau me défendre des choses, vous fatiguez ma résistance, et vous avez une civile opiniâtreté qui me fait venir doucement à tout ce qu'il vous plaît.

Dorimène fears that she might be led to marry Dorante, not for love but because of his elegant "témoignages." She runs the risk of loving the gifts more than the giver. Esthetics and ethics do not necessarily go together, after all. Dorimène's attitude is like that of the princess Ériphile in another entertainment devised for the king, *Les Amants magnifiques*, produced in 1670. Ériphile refuses two princes who woo her with magnificent spectacles, preferring a man of valor whom she loves for his own inherent qualities. She resists the sacrifice of ethical values to esthetic gestures, precisely what remains on Dorimène's mind.

The "civile opiniâtreté" that Dorimène mentions is especially dangerous: the polite esthetic forms conventionally expected from lovers constitute a pressure speciously used to make an ethical point. This is more than a fancy suggestion that Dorimène does not wish to be seduced: she wants above all to preserve her own self-esteem as well as the integrity that her love confers on Dorante. Although she understands the stakes, she knows how hard it is to resist beauty. Dorimène does not want to yield, but realizes that gradually she may, given her human nature and the attractions of beauty.

She objects to the courtship, finally, on two grounds:

> . . . les dépenses que je vous vois faire pour moi m'inquiètent par deux raisons: l'une qu'elles m'engagent plus que je ne voudrais; et l'autre, que je suis sûre, sans vous déplaire, que vous ne les faites point que vous ne vous incommodiez; et je ne veux point cela.

Despite her idealistic desire to remain uncontaminated by materialistic values, Dorimène is "engagée"—obligated by the presents. And she fears that Dorante may bankrupt himself in the process—which would impose the ultimate obligation: marry him to bail him out, as it were! (She is of course unaware of Dorante's borrowing from Jourdain and of his ability to avoid honoring his debts; she never does discover that her Dorante is an avatar of Dom Juan in his relationship with Monsieur Dimanche.) Dorimène wants to remain free, but she is already concerned for Dorante, and aware of it. She is also concerned, however, by her own ethical dilemma. Dorimène, who observes and judges her own behavior, is the play's only character who is not only scrupulously honest but self-conscious about her attitudes and behavior. As she struggles to preserve her values, she risks marrying Dorante not in response to his courtship, but to put an end to it while she may still give her love freely without an overriding sense of obligation. She would accomplish what Jupiter asks of Alcmène: to give to the lover, not to the husband. In order to preserve the freedom of her love, Dorimène must do, paradoxically, as Dorante asks and renounce her liberty.

The audience surely wonders at finding so ethical and virtuous a woman as Dorimène with a wastrel like Dorante. And if these names have any meaning at all, they help set up the surprise, since similar names would be expected to connote like characters. Just as Corneille had used "Dorante" for the *Menteur* who gilds over his shameful identity—preferring the trappings of the swashbuckling, self-reliant hero à la Corneille to his own status as a young man fresh out of Orléans with a degree, perhaps, in law (shades of Molière's own youth!)—Molière's Dorante uses Jourdain's gold to hide his shabby circumstances, while Jourdain uses him to lend luster to his own social situation. Molière may have intended us to assume that Jourdain views Dorimène in the same light: for both *Dor*ante and *Dor*imène are his means toward aristocracy, as if the very gold in their names reflected the ethical substance to which he aspires.

But any such confusion is dispelled once Dorimène appears. Functionally and dramatically, the essence of Dorimène is altruistic, as if her name had been derived from a Greek, not a Latin, etymon: dóron, gift. If Dorante is a gilder, Dorimène is a giver. A hint that this is the connotation Molière intended is provided by the participial forms implicit in the names: Dor*ante* is Latinate, Dori*mène* Greek. The phonemic similarity heightens the effect produced when her character is revealed in stark contrast to Dorante's. It is also perhaps no accident that the plays produced before and after *Le Bourgeois* *gentilhomme* contain settings and characters that are Greek—*Les Amants magnifiques* and *Psyché*: Molière may have had Greek etymons on his mind as a vehicle for representing the nobility of chosen characters like Dorimène and Cléonte (who is the only other person in this play with a Greek-derived name and with the courage to declaim openly his genuine ethical ideals). It turns out, when the significance of her name is considered, that Jourdain was entirely right in choosing Dorimène—and entirely wrong: her genuinely aristocratic ethos transcends the gestures that Dorante produces and Jourdain admires, and condemns the system that would dominate not only her but Jourdain as well.

Jourdain is doubly a dupe and victim, for his futile attempt to convert authentic gold into specious esthetic and ethical substance makes him underestimate and ignore the real integrity of his own character. He indeed does possess qualities and is not just a uni-dimensional bourgeois aping his betters. Intelligence and an ethical sense coexist with his impulse to deny what, after all, is only an accident of birth and fortune. Molière's supreme irony lies in his juxtaposition of Jourdain's genuine merits, worthy of admiration, with his desire to be admired for qualities he can never possess.

Although in comical modes, Molière points up Jourdain's intel-ligence. His version of the note to Dorimène, straightforward *and* précieux, surpasses all the permutations rung on it by the maître de philosophie, whose idiocies, perhaps meant to mock his pupil, ac-tually make Jourdain look clever. To his surprise Jourdain performs without training what he imagines is a courtly accomplishment. He has been speaking prose; his first effort at a billet-doux is perfect: these abilities need no improvement. When his intellectual capacities prove suitable for courting Dorimène, he dismisses the teacher.

In the next scene with the tailor (II, v), Jourdain's common sense and notions of ethical behavior are also in evidence, but the tailor keeps shifting the argument to overcome Jourdain's reasonable ob-jections. The professional artisan's control of material signs of value in the clothing that he is delivering makes Jourdain forget his justified anger with the tailor and overwhelms his good sense. The stockings in fact *are* too tight, the shoes *do* pinch, the flowers *are* upside down. (The stockings are "des bas de soie que j'ai pensé ne mettre jamais," as Jourdain says in I, ii, meaning both that he had never dreamed of wearing such hose *and* that the stockings are so tight he thought he would never be able to get them on.) All his objections pale, however, before the tailor's authoritative praise of his art and atelier: "J'ai chez moi un garçon qui, pour monter une rhingrave, est le plus grand génie du monde." The ceremonial act of dressing Jourdain to music dispels the most serious objection: that the tailor had, unethically, cut his suit from Jourdain's own cloth; the balletic interlude, like those of the music and dancing masters, glorifies the master's view of his profession, celebrates his authority, and cuts short Jourdain's self-interested, although entirely ethical, arguments.

It is odd that Jourdain does not get the better of the tailor, or even his due from him, since they are dealing in "material" values—the pun is intended—all too familiar to this cloth merchant's son (IV, iii). With the philosopher he had seemed surprisingly clever; but in the scene with the tailor, ironically juxtaposed to the pedant's language lesson, Jourdain is made to seem a fool. In a trading situation where he has natural authority—and the experience of a lifetime—Jourdain yields because the esthetic dimension implicit in his notion of aristocracy depends on the tailor's connivance. Thus, he cannot apply realistic standards known through experience and intuition when dealing in goods and services. Unlike Dorimène, he is not concerned with freely bestowed gifts, but with an exchange in which he intends to get his money's worth. He fails, because specious though high-sounding responses by the tailor and the masters violate Jourdain's normal commercial standards as they sell him spurious esthetic gestures.

Jourdain's ethical sense also emerges, and more altruistically at that, during the brawl amongst the masters (II, ii–iii). His spontaneous attempt at peacemaking ends when he recalls that he is wearing a new robe: protecting the beauteous sign of nobility becomes more important than following the civilized wish to separate the combatants. The masters do not much deserve his intervention anyway, the audience may properly feel, since in the crunch they ignore the ethical values they had facetiously ascribed to their arts while currying Jourdain's patronage: music is necessary for "la paix universelle," dance to prevent "un mauvais pas" in the conduct of affairs (I, ii). As Jourdain's real qualities are sacrificed to imaginary values, he is ethically diminished. His own best interests are neutralized by esthetic show: new clothes mean more than getting his money's worth from the tailor or bringing peace to his teachers. And in return for this diminution, ironically, he is paid in worthless currency.

Unlike Jourdain, Dorimène resists the shrinking of her essential worth. If Dorante responds to her agreement to marry him in words that she must take ironically—"Que j'ai d'obligation, Madame, aux soins que vous avez de conserver mon bien. Il est entièrement à vous, aussi bien que mon coeur, et vous en userez de la façon qu'il vous plaira" (V, ii)—her part in the dialectic of obligation is ended. For her response is meant seriously: "J'userai bien de tous les deux." She will marry him before he can purchase her with presents, in a free gift of her own that may create worth where there was none. She would base marriage, the ultimate reconciliation in comedy, on her integrity and on the ethical implications of the one word: "bien." No more diamonds, no more dinner parties. There remains only the "ballet des nations," Jourdain's spectacular entertainment devised for her, which Dorimène can watch at her ease since it no longer can serve to undermine her integrity.

While the plot ends in the traditional manner of New Comedy— exemplified by Menander, his imitators in Rome, the Italian Renaissance and its imitators, Shakespeare—with three pairs of lovers united, the *senex* satisfied, and even his wife approving of the son-in-law, Molière does not conclude the entertainment so simply. The complexity of the "ballet des nations" transcends the glorification of pleasure concluding *Monsieur de Pourceaugnac* (1669) and the ordered pomp of *Les Amants magnifiques*. Nor does it completely parallel the ceremony doctorizing Argan in *Le Malade imaginaire*, to which the Turkish ceremony in act IV is a closer equivalent. Molière could have ended with the triple marriage and a celebration in dance of Jourdain's new dignities. Surely there had already been enough music and dance to satisfy both the king and Lully.

Molière uses the "ballet des nations" to conclude the play thematically, as the triple marriage completes the traditional plot and as the *Mamamouchi* ceremony satisfies Jourdain's fantastic wish for a new identity. While considerably more involved than any earlier musical sequence, the "ballet des nations" is consistent with them. In each previous dance, unreal sets of values were glorified for the sake of one of the masters and finally for Jourdain. The concluding ballet recapitulates the thematics of value implicit in the earlier dances. True to the classical esthetic, Moliere shapes the entertainment so that the unusual ending not only pleases but illuminates the significance of the play as a whole.

The ballet is a self-contained miniature theater piece restating the play's complementary themes: that material means cannot command authentic ethical or esthetic values; that, unless known directly, values remain problematic; and, finally, that only a gift freely bestowed can create value where none exists—the ethical bottom line in each of the comedies examined in these essays. The ballet emerges organically from the plot: originally commissioned to please and to seduce Dorimène, it is put off because of Madame Jourdain's unexpected arrival (IV, ii) until the end, when its full thematic impact can best be felt. It serves as an epilogue spectacle witnessed by an audience of onstage characters: the *Mamamouchi* with his bourgeois household, Cléonte and Covielle in their Turkish disguises, and the aristocrats Dorante and Dorimène.

A prologue, the "première entrée" entitled "Dialogue des gens qui en musique demandent des livres," complicates the play-within-a-play, as three "importuns," two couples "du bel air," two Gascons, a Swiss, and a bourgeois family demand and are refused the program book needed to follow the ballet to be performed. (*Ecce* a quarrel, the dramatic structure *par excellence* of comedy.) The offended bourgeois couple stalk out, but not because they lack the libretto needed to appreciate the scenes sung in foreign languages and a Poitevinaccented French. They are less concerned with experiencing Beauty than with receiving a booklet in recognition of their daughter's beauty. The beautiful, Molière implies, is accessible only to the cultivated—or the aristocrats in the audience.[1]

The structure of the ballet induces analogies between the spectators in the theater, the onstage spectators in Jourdain's home, and the prologue characters, who are a potential audience for *entrées* three through six. Each of these three audiences expects beauty in language and gesture as the artistic equivalent of honorable sentiment—an expectation that recapitulates Jourdain's speech preceding Dorimène's entrance and that Dorimène has led us to suspect. But will the ballet accomplish this and satisfy the Horatian ideal of instruction coupled with pleasure?

The real audience's expectations differ from those both of the ballet-prologue characters and of the onstage witnesses, who are more interested in pleasure than ethics. The audience sees the ballet as epilogue to a play whose dominant theme has been Jourdain's misestimation of aristocratic values and his attempt to purchase them. With the plot settled, the ballet informs us without a libretto that the final representation of Beauty and honest gesture is not on the lofty level that the prologue characters imagine it to be. The ballet represents a series of standard love songs—trivial complaints: again the quarrel—disguised by foreign languages. The ultimate joke is the absence of value. Divining this, the theater audience must savor the irony in the final couplet chanted by everyone on stage: "Quels spectacles charmants, quels plaisirs goûtons-nous! / Les Dieux mêmes, les Dieux n'en ont point de plus doux." The couplet dwells on pleasure with no hint of ethical content, a reminder of the

---

1. It would have made a neat Pirandellian bit *avant la lettre* to distribute libretti at Chambord to the king and his intimates. It makes thematic sense to give program notes to Dorante and Dorimène, and perhaps to the *Mamamouchi* on his demand or on that of the noble couple encouraging his illusion. At the Palais Royal, distributing libretti to members of the audience according to rank, however, would have been impractical and incendiary. Pirandello, sí, Beaumarchais, no.

diverting function of comedy that the play as a whole implicitly undercuts.

While comedy diverts us from our everyday cares and, more seriously, from our fears concerning our shortcomings and lack of authoritative worth, if we understand the comedy properly we will also experience a renewed vision of our own absolute valuelessness even as we laugh at the comic protagonist who would deny his. As we enter the theater expecting to laugh at a character who denies his own identity, we are "diverted" from ourselves as our principal object of attention—along with our failings and whatever fears and instincts we actively repress. But our laughter itself does redirect attention to ourselves, in a way made painless by esthetic pleasure and in the company of others who share the same renewed insight into themselves. A comic catharsis occurs within the spectator who laughs at another's failure to escape the feared vision of his value-lessness, or at his delusion by false images of value foisted upon him. If Molière nearly always leaves us laughing, he has at the same time lanced some of our deepest psychological wounds.

But comedy cannot leave us with nothing but a renewed sense of worthlessness and remain comedy. Like the play's characters, the audience must be reconciled to systems of relative value after the reminder of their contingency, their dependence upon some benef-icent and giving moral force. It is precisely the plays lacking such reconciliation that trouble us most: *Dom Juan, Le Misanthrope, George Dandin, L'École des femmes.*

The mechanism of reconciliation is most elaborate in *Le Bourgeois gentilhomme* and *Le Malade imaginaire*—the triple marriage and the *Mamamouchi* scene; the marriage of Angélique and Cléante, the ex-pulsion of Béline, and the elevation of Argan to the rank of Doctor *honoris causa*. The comédie-ballet seems to have allowed Molière to create a kind of reconciliation for the protagonist that differs from the typical comic mode of reconciliation, for it rests wholly on illusory values taken seriously, conferred through parodistic cere-monies of ritual initiation, and ultimately dependent on some ex-ternal authority such as an order of knighthood or a faculty of medicine. But all reconciliation stems from authority, and, unless it flows from God or king—the ultimate centers of mythology and ideology for Molière's period—authority must remain arbitrary and conventional; so do values associated with social or professional élites, which operate according to their own mythologies erected in imitation of those which govern the culture as a whole.

In comedy, where divinity practically never intervenes (the significant exceptions in Molière's corpus being his *Amphitryon* and *Dom Juan*), a prince most typically brings reconciliation, reminding the characters restored to their senses that none but him possesses absolute value and that they exist relative to one another in a social context. His own sense of responsibility to the divinity whose power and grace he imitates is also emphasized. Shakespeare's great comedies follow such a pattern—one thinks of Theseus, of the prince in that most central work, *Measure for Measure*, of Prospero—and even in *Le Misanthrope* Molière makes a pass at such a reconciliation as the offstage marshals try to bring peace between Alceste and Oronte. Their real failure, despite the apparent success that Philinte recounts, marks Alceste's refusal of any secular authority: only God or the king himself could by a show of naked power, if at all, bring him into line. The king does not mix in Jourdain's affairs, either to ennoble him or to remind him that he is irremediably bourgeois. But the ballet's final couplet, alluding to the gods and, consequently, the king, does suggest that all values ultimately depend on the king, surrogate of the ultimate source of value, God. And the ways of both are mysterious.

Molière understood the philosophical import of divine right theory in the familiar Pascalian terms. In this influential perspective, man could acquire value only through the freely given grace of God in the hereafter, or the bounty of the king in the here and now. In the darker, absolute vision of things, the radical Jansenist vision and the vision of Spinoza, the sole context in which man could sense his worth, and lack of worth, his *grandeur* and his *misère*, was that of the eternal cosmos: *sub specie aeternitatis.*

In the view limited to the here and now, however, the perspective most appropriate to comedy, the king confers value on his chosen and lends meaning to their actions by his love and *bonté*, the royal analogues of divine charity and grace. The final couplet of *Le Bourgeois gentilhomme* implicitly evokes the king to rival the pagan gods—as close a reference as permitted on the stage to the king's divine power. The consequent notion of our dependence on a king–God recalls not only the dominant structure of *Dom Juan*, but Molière's persistent vision from *Le Tartuffe* onward, in which a protagonist questions his value and attempts to persuade himself and others of his absolute worth independent of God's free and arbitrary grace, or the king's favor, or woman's love (Éliante, Elvire, Madame Jourdain, Elmire), or the charity of any of the human analogues of God and king who function (speciously, within the absolute perspective) as arbiters of value among men.

Jourdain's need for the connivance of "professionals"—musicians, cooks, pedants, et al.—as arbiters of worth, a far cry from the king evoked at the ballet's end, suggests how desperate and dependent we can be in the borrowing of our dignities. (Are we not close here to the vision of *King Lear*?) And if, like Jourdain in the play and the bourgeois in the ballet prologue, we would exercise material means (as in buying seats in the theater of ideas, beauty, and ethics) to gain esthetic or ethical values imputed to some idealized élite (the "intellectual establishment," for example), we risk disappointment. For our notions of exclusive groups and their experiences comport more illusion than truth.

We tacitly share a wish, the reflex of the dissatisfaction with our condition that produces this mythology, that Beautiful People without ethical dilemmas must exist—that they should be as we would believe God intended his ultimate creature, the acme of creation before the Fall that, mythological or not, is part and parcel of our being. And we all want admission to the good, beautiful, happy—or privileged—life that we assume they enjoy, to the Isles of the Blessed of ancient mythology and of Aristotle. The system of analogies operating through the "ballet des nations"—audience, onstage audience, prologue audience—helps us acknowledge our own desire to join the Beautiful People, the happy few in a sense Stendhal might perhaps have admitted. It is no accident that Jourdain is Molière's most congenial and accessible character. Nor is it without purpose that Molière does not cancel out Jourdain's final wish fulfillment.

One might argue that the ending, with its reconciliations based on Jourdain's *Mamamouchisation*, fits a comédie-ballet, and that Jourdain is, after all, in a fool's paradise. But ballet serves comedy, despite Lully, and may reinforce serious themes. Molière could have restored Jourdain's sanity in a ballet, or he might have had Jourdain really ennobled by inviting the king to participate directly in the comedy at Chambord. Rather than exorcise Jourdain's desire for identification, Molière perpetuates it, warning, however, that Jourdain's conception of aristocratic values is inaccurate: the essence of nobility lies not in Dorante's "gilding" esthetic gestures but in Dorimène's "giving" grace and ethics. The fancy, and trivial, gestures of the "ballet des nations" derive value only from the fact that the king chooses to honor the performance by his presence, to confer, graciously, his high patronage upon it. The final couplet reminds us of that.

Molière also does not exorcise our desire for freedom from anxieties that keep us from the good life and the happiness that Aristotle poses as the object of man's desire—and of philosophy. We ask comedy to divert us from those concerns, and *Le Bourgeois gentilhomme* evokes that wish right through the emphasis on pleasure in the final couplet, as in the ending of *Monsieur de Pourceaugnac*: "Ne songeons qu'à nous réjouir: / La grande affaire est le plaisir." "Songeons" suggests how much of a dream, a longed-for state, pleasure is. Life here is not like a delightful dream: the objective is to make life conform to what we imagine, or dream, it once was in some mythological past, or might again be in some eschatological future; or is the objective perhaps not to accept life's limitations with all of Philinte's resigned sense of irony? For Molière cautions that our notions of the beautiful and the good may not be accurate; that the Beautiful People may distortedly impersonate, not personify as an accurate reflection, the Idea of the Good; that our mythologies are projections of our psychological needs, weaknesses, desires—as well as of our strengths and confidence. His comedy confronts us with the insubstantiality of our illusions about ourselves and the universe where we would like to think of ourselves as harbored, even while providing some basis for systems of relative value divorced from the absolute vision—the absolute mythology—in which the corollary of God's allness is the nothingness of man. Molière's comedy makes us turn from the void that it has brought to our attention and reconciles us to a less than perfect system of relative values respectful of human needs and institutions, even while it invites us to acknowledge gratefully our dependence on some source of integrity—the Idea of the Good, or God, or king, or Constitution within our own republic—on some free agent of beauty and ethics, on some benign and loving bestower of human value.

INDEX

Adam, Antoine, 136*n*

Alcestis, 125

Alcides, 125

Alexander the Great, as romantic hero and metaphoric figure for Louis XIV, 44

Aristophanes: *Lysistrata*, 133; Old Comedy, 37; verbal fantasy, 4

Aristotle: challenged by Sganarelle in *Dom Juan*, 40; on comedy, 24; definition of dramatic poetry, 6; on "inferior" protagonist of comedy, 11; and Isles of the Blessed, 153; seeks happy life in *Nicomachaean Ethics*, 40, 154

Augustine (Saint): Augustinian assumptions on man's nature and God's love, 65; Augustinian Catholicism practiced by Pascal, 56; *Confessions*, recurrent theme in, 56; *see also* Monica; Mythology, Christian: the Fall

Beaumarchais, Pierre Augustin Caron de, 150*n*

Boccaccio, Giovanni, 136

Boileau-Despréaux, Nicolas, 120

Christian humanism, 52, 82, 123; Molière's, 34

Classicism, 3, 5, 50, 149; moral program of French Classicism, 122; structure, 112; *see also* Comedy, structure of

Comédie-ballet, 2, 151, 154

Comedy: in Aristotle's terms, 24; basis of in *Le Tartuffe*, 24; function of, 8–11,

124, 151, 154–5; in Molière's terms, 8–9; in Platonist terms, 6; pleasure induced in spectator by, 3, 5; problematic nature, exemplified by *L'Avare*, 9–10; reconciliation in, 71; rhythm of, 59, 127, 132; structure of, 1–3, 10, 32, 39, 49, 50, 69, 111, 122, 134–35, 137

Commedia dell'arte all'improviso: influence on Molière, 1, 15, 39, 79; Molière's tribute to in *Les Fourberies de Scapin*, 1

Corneille, Pierre: Aristocratic ideals in, 128; characters in: Auguste, 98, 120, 123–25, César, 123, Chimène, 123–24, Dorante, 145, Horace, 124, Livie, 131, Nicomède, 123, Rodrigue, 123; *Cinna*, source of in Montaigne, 138; conversion in tragedies, 57, 62; dramaturgy, 65, 123–24, 128; heroic tragedy, 122, 135; heroism, 63, 123–24

Dante Alighieri, 55

Don Quixote: its hero and his squire, 70; shaped by baroque doctrine, 92

Epicureanism: Molière's, 34; as source of French moral thought, 123

Epicurus, 97–98

Fabliaux, tradition of comic tale, 136

Farce, in Molière's plays, 1, 2, 16, 51, 61–62, 67, 79, 115–16, 127, 130, 136

Freud, Sigmund, 7

Fronde, 81, 128